Mme Louis LANGEVIN
1886 - 1956

CITY FARMHOUSE STYLE

DESIGNS FOR A MODERN COUNTRY LIFE

KIM LEGGETT

PRINCIPAL PHOTOGRAPHY BY ALISSA SAYLOR

ABRAMS, NEW YORK

CONTENTS

Enrique Olvera
at home in the whole food kitchen
POLPO
Breakstone's
CREAM CHEESE
BREAKSTONE'S
CREAM CREST
BREAKSTONE'S
NEW ENGLAND

FOREWORD

◀ There's a simplicity to farmhouse staples that helps them play well with other design elements and aesthetics, whether your tastes veer toward the modern, traditional, or somewhere in between.

CHALK IT UP TO THE UBIQUITOUS FARM-TO-TABLE TREND, BUT IT seems that anything branded with the word "farmhouse" is suddenly having a moment—from simple white farmhouse kitchens to amber-hued farmhouse ales. Farmers, of course, were doing "farm-to-table" far before it became the hyphenate du jour on highfalutin city menus, and those same farming folk knew the merits of, say, a wide-bowl apron sink or easy-access open shelving well before those items became staples of designer portfolios and home décor catalogs.

The real beauty of farmhouse style—unlike other more fleeting design trends—is that it's rooted in roll-up-your-sleeves practicality. Farmhouses have been around for hundreds of years, after all, and they were designed to work hard—to accommodate multigenerational families, feed a crowd, and, yes, handle a little dirt.

As the editor in chief of *Country Living*, a brand with design-loving readers all over the country, I've seen firsthand how the demand for all things farmhouse has grown exponentially over the past few years—and well beyond the county lines of honest-to-goodness farm towns. Farmhouse style seems to resonate everywhere, from the neon lights of Times Square to one-stoplight town squares, and for good reason: A farmhouse table or an apron sink work just as well in an urban loft or suburban Tudor as they do in a country farmhouse.

I also suspect farmhouse style has such widespread appeal because it's inherently inviting. It's warm, welcoming, and, thanks to its adaptability, all-inclusive. At *Country Living*, we run across hundreds of objectively beautiful spaces every month, but our most important criteria when vetting homes is this: Does it make you want to fidget, or does it make you want to linger? If it's the former, it falls into the "no" pile. A farmhouse-inspired home, if done right, certainly doesn't make you want to fidget. Nothing about farmhouse style is too precious, too sleek, too hard-lined, or too cold.

It's no surprise, then, that Kim Leggett, the brilliant design mind behind the lifestyle brand, blog, and boutique City Farmhouse (and author of this very book), has helped plant and grow the seeds of the farmhouse-style movement. Yes, she has an incredible eye for good design, but perhaps more important, she embodies the warm, open, friendly aesthetic of the farmhouse look. Our paths first crossed at a *Country Living* fair event several years ago, where, after I likely spent too much money in her perfectly curated booth, we started talking and realized that we both hail from the same small farming town nestled in the northwest corner of Tennessee. Maybe it's because the muddy water of the Mississippi is thicker than blood, but Kim immediately felt like family. But here's the thing: I suspect she has that "you're one of my people" effect on pretty much everyone, and therein lies her personal sit-and-stay-awhile charm.

That sense of personal connection is another check mark in favor of farmhouse style, isn't it? At the risk of sounding a little "crotchety old man," I've found that modern-day social media connections simply can't compete with a sprawling front porch that fosters impromptu (in-person!) conversations with your neighbors or a long farmhouse table designed for sit-down Sunday suppers. Even other hallmarks of farmhouse style—family heirlooms, cleverly upcycled accents—are intended to connect us with the past. Creaky hardwood floors remind us of those who walked before us, as do the resourcefully repurposed items that decorate our planked walls and open shelves. (Now, if only someone could come up with a clever way to repurpose a Mason jar . . .)

An aesthetic movement that not only values but also *celebrates* all things old, chipped, and weathered is pretty much destined to have longevity. Twenty years from now, you may question that chevron wallpaper or those ikat draperies, but you won't regret a cast-iron claw-foot tub or an heirloom-worthy iron bedframe. Farmhouse style is time-tested. It has staying power. You can bet the farm on it.

—RACHEL HARDAGE BARRETT, editor in chief, *Country Living*

▶ Farmhouse style is the design equivalent of "sit and stay awhile."

INTRODUCTION

I WAS RAISED BY MY GRANDMOTHER IN A SMALL TENNESSEE TOWN of mostly long-standing farming families or blue-collar workers. The homes that made up our neighborhood were centered around a textile factory—the cotton mill, as it was known by the locals—and were built to house the many laborers who made their living there. The architectural exteriors were designed as bungalows of sorts; all had a front porch and large picture windows. The dwellings were small, composed of only two bedrooms, but each had a space reserved for a dining room. We were close with our neighbors—meaning they were only a few feet away and friendly.

I grew up in the 1960s when retro design was all the rage. Pea greens, yellows, reds, and oranges showed up in everything from fabrics to wallpapers, carpeting to furnishings. Chrome dining sets ordered from the Sears, Roebuck and Company "wish book" appeared in every kitchen up and down the street, including our own. The popular color of the day was red, but my grandmother chose gray. There was a reason behind that: She was a style leader, not a follower. While our neighbors were painting their walls vibrant colors, she was painting hers white. And, while just across the street, mill worker Mrs. Cash, the local schoolteacher Mrs. Bell, and the seamstress Mrs. Waller were proudly showing off their new orange and green sofas, Minnie Ola'Belle Harness (my grandmother) was upholstering hers in a tapestry of various shades of cream. Our seating didn't come from a catalog or the local furniture store. It was a 1930s tattered and torn Duncan Phyfe–style castoff found one Friday night at the local

▶ Farmhouse style is born out of our love for the past and a desire to live a comfortable, more laid-back lifestyle.

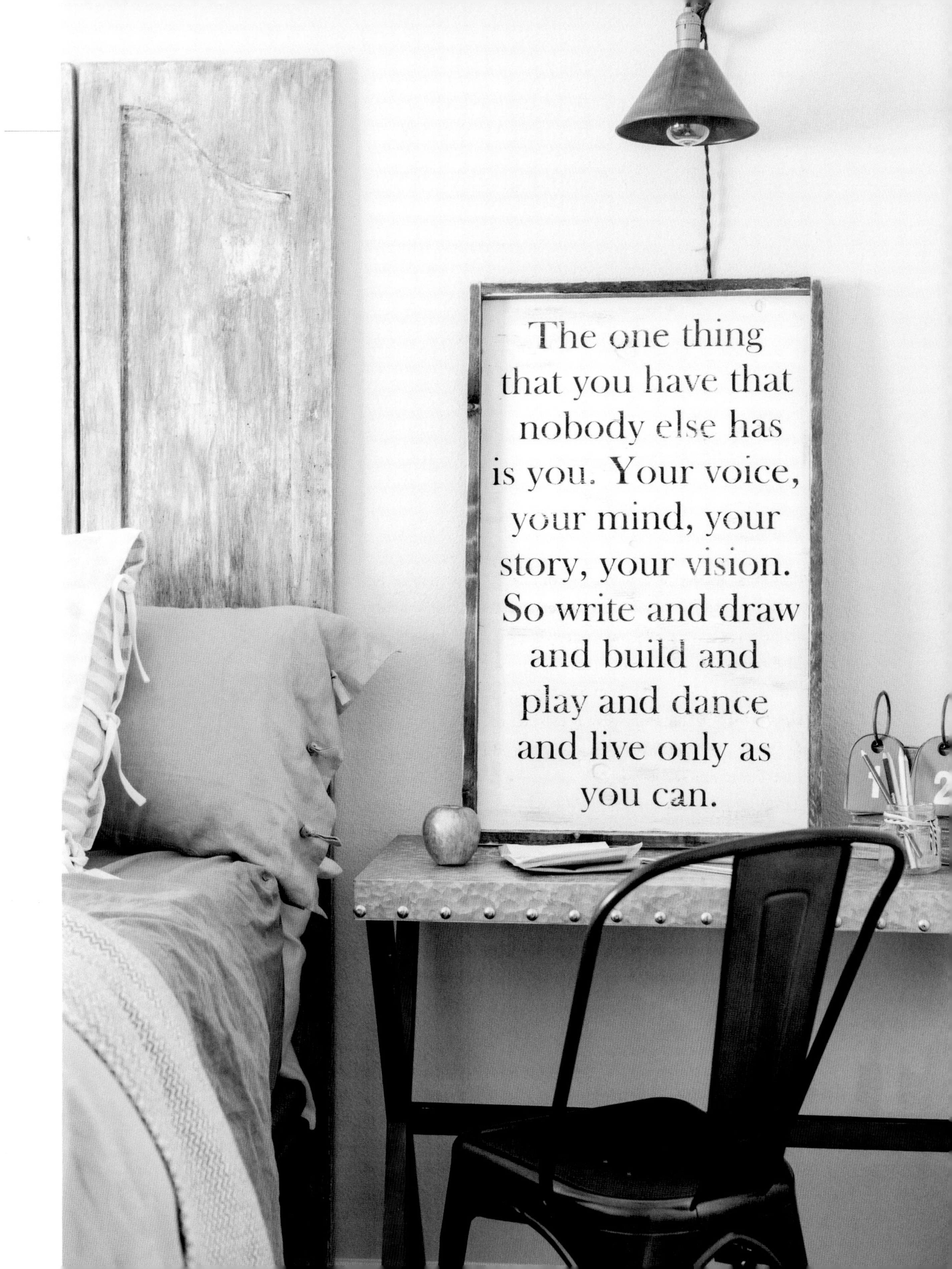
The one thing
that you have that
nobody else has
is you. Your voice,
your mind, your
story, your vision.
So write and draw
and build and
play and dance
and live only as
you can.

Peppermint Pond Auction. My bedroom suite was a hand-me-down from my grandmother's oldest daughter, my aunt Juanita. It was an antique, made of oak, and barely holding together. The golden surface was worn, and not in a pretty way, but Momma, as I called my grandmother, went to work making it look good as new—in an old sort of way. She painted it white and distressed it so that its golden, worn surface peeked through. While our house looked nothing like the trendy homes along the street, our neighbors often remarked that it was the most beautiful.

Holiday gatherings took place in the crowded dining room, with odd chairs pulled up for seating so that everyone could be together. Although the table was small, it held an abundance of food, which always included my grandmother's chicken and dressing. When she and my grandfather moved from the farm, they purchased the dining room set for their new "city" home. Along with the table, it included a buffet and a china cabinet. The old sideboard was my favorite, not because it held rows of homemade pies and cakes during the holidays but because it had a silverware drawer, which wasn't really a place for storing silver at all. I called it the "junk drawer," and oh, what a variety of fabulous trinkets it held. I rifled through it often, scavenging bits and bobbles of curiosities that made their way straight to my bedroom. It never occurred to me until I was grown up that Momma likely spiced it up just for me.

The house sat on a tiny plot of land, just a few steps from the street, but it was surrounded with the most stunning array of blooms—red azaleas, big snowballs of blue hydrangeas, and the annuals that Momma would add to the beds each spring. She and my grandfather were fortunate to have a tiny spot out back for growing fresh vegetables. And the garden yielded enough each summer for farm-to-table meals, or backyard-to-table in our case, and canning for the winter. Momma and Aunt Sue made their own sauerkraut from the fresh cabbage grown in the patch. It was fermented in a ten-gallon stoneware crock that I have today.

Although money was tight, and repurposing old worn-out pieces was certainly resourceful, I don't believe that's why my grandmother chose to decorate that way. I believe it was more about originality and comfort and creating something that comes from the soul and the hands. I don't remember that she ever referred to it as any certain "style"—it was simply home. She made use of every inch of her tiny home place, including the yard, creating beauty in all that surrounded her and leaving nothing to waste.

When I grew up and moved away from the place that I had called home, I took my grandmother's imagination, creativity, and reinvention with me to a tiny little apartment in the center of town. To style it, I sought out old pieces with a storied past, mismatched tables and chairs, odd fragments that hung on the wall, and scraps that were never intended to be part of home décor in the first place. Just like Momma's house, it was a simple and comfortable space with no real design "label." I came to appreciate it as more of a lifestyle than a formal definition of decorating. Such is the character of farmhouse style today.

In cities all across America a movement in the way we style our homes is taking shape. The beauty of farmhouse style is that it recognizes no boundaries. It embraces an eclectic mix of periods and aesthetics, combining the traditional farmhouse of decades ago with modern trends of today. Oil-burning lamps have been replaced with crystal chandeliers and industrial factory lighting, antique doors have become creative passageways, old mercantile signs are now prized objets d'art, and cupboards and pie safes once reserved for the farmhouse kitchen have taken on new life as modern-day centerpieces of a room—maintaining their storage function but newly revered as cherished discoveries. Even our gardens and porches are reminiscent of the farmhouse landscape, featuring creative displays of rusty discarded elements of the farm repurposed for the way we live today.

This book is written as a home tour of sorts, showcasing the many brilliant ways that homeowners across the United States have interpreted the style in their own homes and lives. It is my hope that after reading these chapters, you'll be inspired to create your own *City Farmhouse Style*, no matter where you call home—whether it is an industrial loft or apartment, a tiny cottage, a brownstone in the city, or a new build in a contemporary neighborhood. And just in case you're having a little trouble finding all that timeworn goodness to create the look, I've thrown in an entire chapter dedicated to my favorite pickin' haunts.

Now, go . . . be inspired . . . create . . . reinvent . . . and come home to the simple beauty of *City Farmhouse Style*.

XO

—KIM LEGGETT

CHAPTER 1

FARMHOUSE INSPIRATION

Designing your home is a lot like falling in love. Before you can wrap your heart and soul around a space, you need to feel an emotional attachment to it. When the look of an old worn cupboard, the faded hues of centuries-old wallpaper, or the nubby textures of homespun fabrics tug at your heartstrings, that's love speaking to you in the form of farmhouse inspiration.

◀ If you have found that you have a genuine love of the past, then follow your dream to make farmhouse style a part of your home.

In the world of design, many things are beautiful. You can appreciate various styles and periods, but when you long to bring a particular look home and build a lifestyle around it, then you've truly found *your* style. This love affair (and inspiration to create) never really ends. It is a constant journey of searching, reinventing, and finding inspiration all over again.

When you are inspired, your desire to learn increases. There's no better teacher than your own eye. Study old pieces you are attracted to and look closely at how they are constructed: Examine whether they are finely crafted or lovingly made by the untrained hand. Feel the surfaces and take in the authentic experience of objects that are worn by a storied past. Over time, you will not only have a better understanding of the things you love but also a deeper appreciation for their age, their past, and the hand that created them.

THE WAY WE WERE

THE RURAL FARMHOUSE: NOTHING TELLS THE story of America's past quite like it. More than just a shelter, it was the heart of the farming family and the central workplace for cooking, canning, churning, and a multitude of other tasks that supported family, field hands, and the farming lifestyle. Most country farmhouses had a simple layout: a kitchen, a front room or parlor for the celebrations of life—engagements, weddings, christenings, baptisms, and reunions—and bedrooms, which were usually small. Because farm families were often large, it was common for several siblings to share a room.

Today, our idea of the old farmhouse is fragmented: It comes to us through salvaged (and discarded) remnants and in collections of vintage pieces that we find along the way. To have the opportunity to literally step back in time to study an authentic farmhouse in its original state is rare. Thanks to conservators of the past like Chris and Laurie Popp, an 1890s Gothic Revival farmhouse in Tennessee stands to tell its story. Original painted beadboard, wallpaper, hardwood floors, and architectural elements remain intact as a testament to all that is authentically farmhouse style. They inspire a passionate desire to salvage, to search out, to renew, to transform, to gather, and to rebuild the past in our own homes.

The Popps raise Cheviot sheep on the farm, using sustainable practices borrowed from past generations. Laurie, a well-known folk artist, uses the wool from her flock in her fiber sculptures. The sheep graze freely on pastures that Laurie says are pure and chemical-free. It's all part of the authentic beauty of the old homeplace.

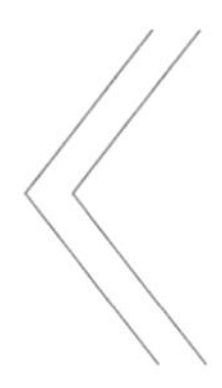

A primitive farm bench squares off with the curves of a Victorian sofa for a simple study in beauty and contrast. The Popps were able to save one large section of the original wallpaper, which was applied over yellow-painted beadboard. Traditionally, cotton or muslin was used as a liner to fill gaps in paneling before decorative paper was applied.

Early-twentieth-century wallpaper featured delicate patterns and soft colors that were more in line with the farmhouse aesthetic than with gaudy Victorian styles. Wallpaper was hand-painted, block-printed, stenciled, and, starting in the late 1700s, machine-printed on rolls of paper using new manufacturing methods. You can still find vintage wallpaper rolls (many sources are online).

You may find a few mechanical issues as you dig for architectural gold, but that's the price we pay when we trade a newly built structure for a house with a past. The Popps stripped out old wiring that had been cobbled together over the years and, in a surprise move, for the most part they didn't replace it! Instead, candle chandeliers and sconces flicker with candlelight and kerosene lamps create a soft glow. For Laurie, illuminating rooms the old-fashioned way makes the atmosphere truly authentic.

An old photograph is an ode to the people who paved the way for this house . . . and for all of us, really. It shows the family of Andrew H. Chamber, a prominent mill owner and the pioneer and original owner of the property.

Running counter to contemporary tastes for manufactured, uniform goods, farmhouse style prizes the unique character of things collected over time: Pieced together from heirlooms and individual finds, this mismatched silverware serves up that kind of humble history, born of necessity.

◀ Testament to the fact that this is still a working farm, and a viable way of life, the corner of the dining room is filled with traditional baskets, still used to gather the raw wool sheared from the Popps sheep, before it is cleaned, carded, and spun into yarn. Laurie sells her wool in one-ounce balls, mostly to farmhouse enthusiasts who display the rolled wool in baskets and antique dough bowls.

▼ The authentic beauty of an old farmhouse comes from things being handmade—and repaired with what is at hand—rather than purchased in a store. Current case in point: Laurie replaced the worn-out rush seats of these ladder-back chairs with her own braided and felted wool. In the past, chair seats were often repaired with rope, jute, or leather straps.

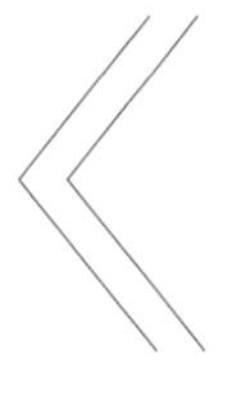

As the middle class grew in number and economic success during the nineteenth and twentieth centuries, the piano (and piano lessons) became more affordable—and piano playing, more popular as a pastime. During this period, many musical scores were written for two players, seated side by side: The piano was useful for courtship, since the piano bench was an acceptable place for a couple to sit (cozily) together yet within earshot of other members of the household.

WHEN WALLS DO TALK . . . ABOUT PAINT

BEFORE THE WIDESPREAD use of factory-made paints at the turn of the twentieth century, paint was mixed by hand using coarsely ground pigment—ochre yellows, iron-oxide reds, and copper-oxide greens—and linseed oil. The finish did not dry evenly, and the coarse brushes early painters used left striated brush marks and a decorative finish that is almost impossible to duplicate today. If you aren't lucky enough to have these historic painted finishes in your own home, shop for sections of wall paneling from salvage or antique dealers. Or you can mimic the appearance by using modern-day ground pigments (mixed into paint) and distressing to achieve a faux aged look. (Unearthed Paints, Earth Pigments, Amy Howard Home Toscana Milk Paint, and Miss Mustard Seed Milk Paint are excellent choices for quality pigments and each have options for blending.)

▼ Nothing quite compares to the humble, handcrafted beauty of a true farmhouse antique. This highchair seat was made from the slats and bottom of a crate; the legs are stripped and hand-whittled hickory branches. Today we call this folk art; back then, it was called rural resourcefulness.

▶ Did you know that a burlap-swaddled Mason jar is the make-do ancestor of the thermos? Burlap is made from loosely woven jute, a plant fiber with insulating properties. Just as in modern thermos design, the burlap insulated a central container (usually a glass jar) and helped keep drinks warm or cold.

Before cast-iron stoves took over, the kitchen fireplace was a necessity for warmth and for whipping up a hot meal. This one is constructed of hand-hewn stone found on the property. It includes a large stone lintel cross section above the hearth for structural stability.

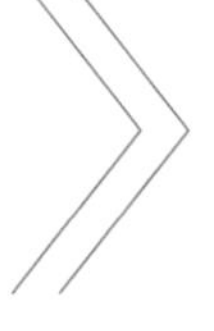

◀ Nothing bolsters a room's farmhouse charm like ticking. A cotton fabric with a familiar striped pattern, ticking is popular for upholstery, throw pillows, aprons, even curtains. But back in the day (way back, in fact; the pattern has been in evidence for at least a thousand years), the sturdy, woven twill had a specific duty: bundling feathers into soft pallets and pillows for sleeping. Since rural folk stuffed their bedding with chicken feathers rather than soft, luxurious goose down, tightly woven ticking kept the sharp feather shafts from poking through. When mass-produced mattresses became an option, manufacturers still chose inexpensive, über-durable ticking as a covering, which is why the fabric is often called mattress ticking.

▶ In farmhouses, every bit of space was needed—and used. Owing to the roof pitch, second-floor bedroom windows are installed near the floor to keep the space cool, just as they are in attics. This one offers a sweet backdrop for a circa-nineteenth-century Tennessee handcrafted child's chair and a tea set dating to the 1940s.

Wearing a well-worn layer of wallpaper, the utilitarian crate at the foot of the bed is a perfect example of repurposing. While the old piece was originally used for the shipping of goods, a resourceful farmhouse wife has turned it into a beautiful clothes storage chest.

The thread and fabric (including fragments from an American flag) in this quilt date to the post–Civil War era, when settlers were anxious to show their patriotism. The quilt's bright cherry fabric—called "turkey red"—was especially popular at the time and was achieved through hand-dyeing with ground up Rubia plant roots.

FARMHOUSE PAINTS

WHEN IT COMES TO DECORATING YOUR home in farmhouse style, one of the most important decisions you'll make is what color to paint the walls. If you are considering "just plain white," then you are among the majority of both amateur and professional home designers who look to this pure and simple color as a favorite choice. Thanks to the popularity of white paint in home decorating, manufacturers have cleverly concocted an ever-growing range of choices; in fact, the sheer variety of shades and tints can sometimes make selecting the best one for your space a real challenge. Spin the white color wheel and you'll discover there's just the right white for creating almost any mood. But before you grab a bucket and whitewash the entire house, here are a few things you should know about this well-loved hue.

FARMHOUSE PAINTS

Choose an organic tone (like Benjamin Moore's Classic Gray) as a backdrop to highlight textures, including weathered wood and stone, and for kitchens with concrete countertops.

If you have large windows and lots of strong light, tone down the brilliance with a gray white (like Valspar's White Pepper). Likewise, if you have a room that gets little sunlight, a simple white paint (like Sherwin-Williams's Pearly White or Benjamin Moore's Simply White) will optimize the light.

Painting a room bright white and filling it with all-white furnishings and accessories can feel too sterile. Opt for a creamy white (like Valspar's Dove White) instead.

For kitchens, ivory (like Benjamin Moore's Ivory White) provides just the right warmth. It looks like pure white without feeling cold.

For a room that is large and rustic, off-white (like Benjamin Moore's Snowfall White) is a warm and inviting choice.

Because white amplifies light, it has a natural ability to maximize space, making a small room or home seem larger than it really is. The brightest of whites (like Valspar's Ultra White) will do the job here. It is also ideal as a clean, uncluttered canvas for artwork, antiques, and gallery displays.

What about blue? The good news is that blue is a perfect farmhouse color, too! And when you paint your porch ceiling with this cool color, it works double-duty to shoo away the haints (or so the legend goes). A haint is a spirit or ghost who has yet to move on to their final resting place. According to old-timers, haints believe the color blue is water, and since they cannot cross water, they are fooled into staying away.

Many regions have their own version of the spirit-deterring "authentic" Haint Blue—hues range from light to dark blue and include some with strong hints of green, depending on the place you call home. But whether you want to protect your home from the elements or the spirits, go with the blue that is the most pleasing to your eye.

FARMHOUSE WALLPAPERS

BY THE LATE 1700s, WHEN NEW PRINTING processes made way for wallpapers to be printed by the roll, a decorative material once available only to the wealthy was suddenly within reach of everyday folk. Practically overnight wallpaper became a trend that spanned all economic levels and was as much a part of setting up housekeeping as buying a bed. Like earlier block-printed examples, the machine-printed papers often mimicked more expensive wall coverings such as tapestries, elaborate murals, and painted florals. Rural homes favored wallpaper that looked like calico and other popular fabrics of the day, and it was celebrated for much more than its good looks. It served as a decorative insulator that sealed up drafty cracks in plank and beadboard walls and ceilings. By the time the twentieth century rolled around, wallpaper had established itself as the most popular decorating element of the era.

Like most trends, wallpaper disappeared for a while, but recently it has rolled back into style. Nothing impacts a room like wallpaper. Unlike back in the day, when it was used simply as a wall covering, it is now showing up in unexpected places—framed as artwork, lining a bookcase, and even decoupaged onto furniture. It serves well as an art installation, whether a single panel or feature wall, too. In the spirit of trying something new, forgo freshening up your farmhouse space with paint and opt for wallpaper instead (on the page that follows are some reasons you'll be glad you did).

BOOK No 5
KAYSER & ALLMAN
MANUFACTURERS OF
WALL PAPERS
PHILADELPHIA
NEW YORK
CHICAGO
MINNEAPOLIS
ESTABLISHED
1871

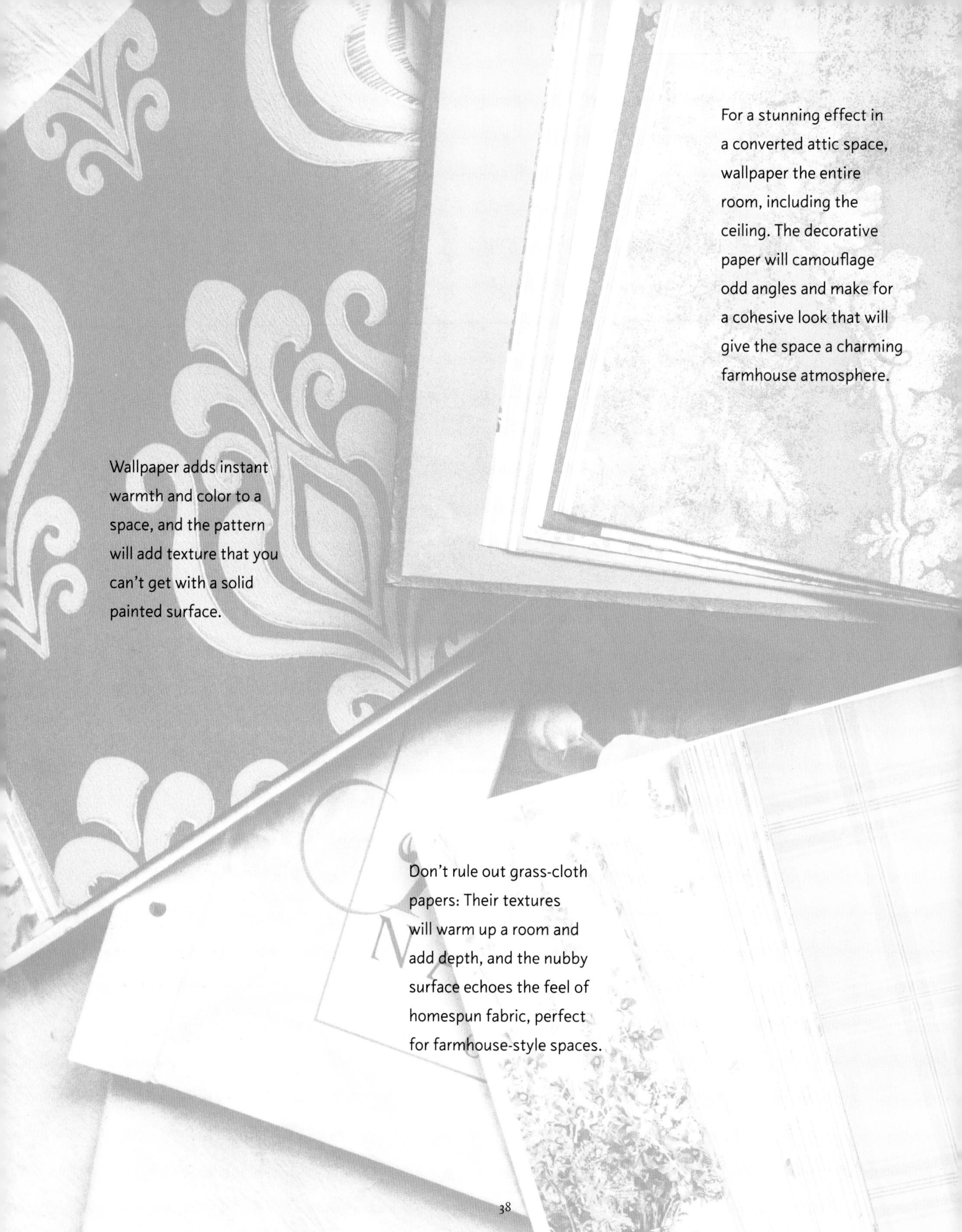

For a stunning effect in a converted attic space, wallpaper the entire room, including the ceiling. The decorative paper will camouflage odd angles and make for a cohesive look that will give the space a charming farmhouse atmosphere.

Wallpaper adds instant warmth and color to a space, and the pattern will add texture that you can't get with a solid painted surface.

Don't rule out grass-cloth papers: Their textures will warm up a room and add depth, and the nubby surface echoes the feel of homespun fabric, perfect for farmhouse-style spaces.

Wall coverings with a neutral background and a larger single motif will show best in lofts and modern farmhouses with high or vaulted ceilings. In small spaces, or rooms broken up with lots of doors and windows, opt for miniature prints that give the room a feeling of intimacy. These small patterns work well in rooms with plank or beadboard, too.

No kitchen design says farmhouse like open shelving. But if eliminating those traditional cabinets isn't an option, then you can easily mimic the look by removing the cabinet doors and lining the interior with a wallpaper backdrop.

FARMHOUSE TEXTILES

FADED, CRUMPLED, WRINKLED, AND FRAYED—such is the hallmark of vintage textiles. The imperfections earned through the passage of time speak to us and are the reason such fabrics are so desirable in farmhouse-style decorating. And it's not just their good looks that draw us in; it's their humble beginnings, their homespun charm, their tiny hand stitching and the purpose behind it: to make clothing, to be slept on, to cover furnishings, to decorate tables and windows, and to serve a host of other simple, everyday uses.

Today, we use vintage textiles in similar ways, but we prize them most as a decorative element: Nothing warms up a home quite like the texture of a vintage handmade fabric. And because so much of this fabric was woven for everyday use, there is a great variety still available to us. One of its many charms is that it blends so well: Because vintage fabrics have a beautiful aged appearance, you can easily mix stripes, like ticking, with solids, like linen.

Speaking of linen, it's one of the most popular vintage textiles for interior design today. Because it's both beautiful and versatile, linen is particularly suited to the comfortable farmhouse style. Just as in times past, it shows up in many décor applications, from upholstered seating to bedding, from window dressings to pillows.

Even in their old age, vintage fabrics hold up pretty well owing to their utilitarian nature and most, including linen, can be handwashed. In fact, linen is the most durable natural fabric there is (it has been around for more than four thousand years. It's one of the oldest known weavings and even appears in the Bible). The secret to preserving the longevity of any vintage textile is to mend any holes and rips right away. Patches from mending are, in their own right, desired and even sought after.

In recent years vintage textiles, especially linen, have made their way onto the runway, showing up in clothing for both women and men, and into bags and accessories. The many shades of natural colors and textures are both comfortable and pleasing to the eye, making them just as desirable for wearing as for use in home décor.

Various patterns of early French and American ticking, grain sacks, and printed plaid and check fabrics lie in wait to take on new life in the modern farmhouse of today. Grain sacks, a popular fabric among farmhouse enthusiasts, are often repurposed into bolsters

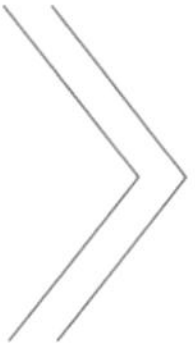

and instantly add country charm to any bed, whether it is a vintage or contemporary one. Printed fabrics (especially blue), once used to dress the simple folk, are now prized as table coverings in country kitchens.

CHAPTER 2

THE UPTOWN CITY FARMHOUSE

APARTMENT, LOFT, BROWNSTONE & COTTAGE LIVING

That all rural farmhouses are spacious rambling structures situated on large plots of land is actually a romanticized modern myth. For decades the farmhouses of tenant farmers—families who could not afford a large farm and rented land in return for a portion of the harvest—have dotted the countryside.

◀ Today, the farmhouse look is right at home in tight quarters and in the heart of bustling cities.

These humble farmhouse dwellings provide just enough space for the essentials of daily living. In recent years, it has become popular to restore these houses and transform them into rural getaways.

But who says you have to own a country house to experience farmhouse charm? From Manhattan lofts and Brooklyn brownstones to Hollywood cottages and homes on the Long Island shore, farmhouse style is showing up *big* with down-home spirit.

THE MODERN FARMHOUSE

"AUTHENTIC" FARMHOUSE STYLE IS often associated with abundant collections overflowing from every nook and cranny, but a minimalist approach can be equally captivating. This simplified, no-fuss look embraces classic architecture, utilitarian pieces, and the everyday beauty of uncomplicated design.

The less-is-more approach is just what Odette Williams and her husband, Nick Law, had in mind when they set out to renovate a historic brownstone in the heart of bustling Brooklyn, New York. The couple dreamed of a space that would evoke the soul of a nineteenth-century farmhouse, even though their home is smack-dab in the middle of one of the world's busiest cities.

With crisp white walls, humble finishes, and carefully curated furnishings, you too can transform a modern dwelling, like this brownstone, into an airy space with a modern spin on farmhouse style. To start, you may have to do some digging to find hidden architectural gems. While restoring the brownstone, Odette peeled back layers of unsightly linoleum (it wasn't the good kind) to unearth gorgeous heart pine floors. Since a minimal farmhouse look is all about letting simple details shine, she opted to forgo area rugs and let the wide-plank floors command center stage.

When designing with this aesthetic, it is important to choose furnishings that have simple, strong features. Here, a streamlined sectional

sofa in a neutral fabric anchors the living room (in uncluttered quarters, tufted upholstery offers more visual interest than a smooth surface treatment).

To create a similar look in your city space, follow Odette's easy styling techniques:

1. Add a pop of color to a neutral space by accessorizing with dramatic hues. Notice how the bold pink in the sofa pillows extends to the antique trunk turned coffee table, where a book cover in the exact tone balances the eye-catching hue.

2. In a design that embraces white space and ample light, strike a homey balance with comfortable seating, like these streamlined chairs inspired by a nineteenth-century French design.

3. In lieu of tables, repurpose an interesting reclaimed object, such as the metal storage trunk used here. Small vintage butcher blocks, stacked wooden boxes, old suitcases, and unusual stools work well, too.

COOK IT UP FARMHOUSE STYLE

WHETHER THEY ARE OLD OR new, in the city or in the honest-to-goodness country, farmhouse kitchens have always been about preparing wholesome hearty meals that nourish the body and the soul. This is why, if you're renovating your own cook space, you might consider a vintage stove with built-to-last beauty: Fixer-uppers are readily available (antiqueappliances.com is an excellent source), as are fully restored models.

For something a little more up to date, Aga, Big Chill, La Cornue, and Elmira Stove Works produce brand-new stoves with classic looks. Odette's kitchen is anchored with a cast-iron Aga that weighs in at more than five hundred pounds and measures an impressive five feet long!

As an added plus—with a statement-making range in place, you can go simple on the cabinetry: At right, a basic Shaker style complements the overall look.

AGA
AGA

▲ Most homeowners feel that long narrow spaces are a design challenge. But if you choose the right furnishings, you can move through the room with ease, and enjoy the added pleasure of a gallery atmosphere. Here, Odette paired a narrow farm table with an interesting mix of diminutive mismatched chairs.

▶ A marble mantel, salvaged from a condemned townhouse in New York's West Village, is just the right scale for the room. Its slim, sculptural shape makes it as much an art form as a practical firebox surround. Flanking the fireplace are custom bookshelves that reach to the top of the brownstone's high ceilings.

THE ART BOX
THE PHOTO BOOK
SPYMASTER
SPIKE MILLIGAN
DESIGN BROOKLYN
WES ANDERSON
THE ICONIC
TIBOR
THE ENDLESS CITY
WORLD

NDIA
COOK BOOK
1.5KG
MORO EAST
Classic Plus

◀ Odette salvaged this striking antique from a favorite junking spot in Williamsburg, New York, and uses it to show off a collection of old-fashioned kitchenware and serving pieces. Look for vintage cabinets with large glass doors to show off collections of your own.

▲ Classic pie tins make perfect farmhouse décor. In the 1950s, these aluminum tins were returnable and bakeries reused them, unlike the disposable variety we know today. Treasure hunt for examples with great logos, like the "New England Flaky Crust Pie" tin shown here.

Finding beauty in the everyday is a hallmark of farmhouse style. In this home, the master bathroom is a space for utilitarian elegance (as opposed to the over-the-top opulence of many master suites). To achieve this look in your own home, choose understated finishes such as subway tile, nickel hardware, and cast-iron sinks. Add baskets for storage; they are the perfect catchall. These timeless choices will create a space that looks equally at home in a turn-of-the-century farmhouse or a modern-day version of one.

In a bedroom, create minimalist farmhouse style with a neutral palette and lots of texture. The cornerstone for such a look can be an upholstered headboard in a natural, nubby fabric. To add interest, pile on the pillows. For a fun twist, mix ticking stripes and asymmetrical embroidery—and update the traditional farmhouse quilt by reaching for a gray-and-white, Aztec-inspired pattern, as Odette does here.

Colorful, pattern-filled rooms may be the modern standard for kids' rooms, but why not share some old-fashioned charm with the little ones in your life instead? The key to success in a farmhouse-style kids room is keeping everything to scale—small scale, that is. Be on the lookout for rustic fixtures and furniture that may have been used in schoolhouses and summer camps. Odette's children's bathroom is equipped with a trough sink that came from an old elementary school.

For a showstopping focal point in your master suite, look no further than an antique claw-foot tub. Few fixtures evoke farmhouse style more than these turn-of-the-century masterpieces—plus, they never go out of style. To score your own, check out local architectural salvage yards or flea markets.

MAKE IT FARMHOUSE STYLE

MAP OUT YOUR STYLE

If you want to chart a stylish, historic look, consider adorning your walls with vintage maps, even well-worn ones. Whether you opt for a framed display or old-school pull-down versions, maps bring appealing color and texture into a room without overpowering the space. Combine design and sentiment with maps depicting places of significance, such as a home state or a honeymoon destination. Here, Odette hung an old schoolhouse map of her native Australia for a striking and nostalgic display.

IT'S ALL IN THE ARCHITECTURAL DETAILS

If you have a historic home and are going for a less-is-more farmhouse look, keep the focus on the architectural details that attracted you to the property in the first place. In other words, steer clear of grand antiques and focus your time and budget on the bones of the home. In Odette's brownstone, the stately staircase that connects the two floors is the crown jewel. The winding focal point was masterfully rebuilt, with new treads installed and the original handrails, balusters, and newel post all restored. The latter was finished with a gleaming mahogany stain that creates a smart contrast with the honey-hued floors. To highlight the impressive millwork, Odette kept the stairwell walls crisp, white, and unadorned.

HUNTER
HUNTER
HUNTER
HUNTER

TUCKED-AWAY CHARM

FULFILLING THE AMERICAN DREAM OF OWNING a home may not be immediately on your radar. But living in a rental doesn't mean you have to sacrifice style: The key is to decorate as if it's your own.

Allison Murphy achieved a perfect farmhouse look in her 1,100-square-foot apartment without changing the existing palette she inherited with the rental. Located in the downtown district of historic Florence, Alabama, and housed in a former furniture warehouse, the two-bedroom tri-level dwelling is tucked within an alleyway and sandwiched between a commercial office space and a sign shop. Although its industrial design elements—exposed brick walls, cement floor, and high ceilings—may seem the opposite of farmhouse style, Allison found they made a perfect backdrop for her collection of farmhouse antiques and contemporary furnishings.

When faced with the limited options of a rental (and its existing walls, floors, and structure), the furnishings you select are the essential tools for building a farmhouse look. For instant country charm, start with a statement piece of furniture and build around it. Allison chose to anchor her living room with a circa-1800s wardrobe. This farmhouse staple would once have been used for storing clothing (before closets became the norm), but Allison uses hers as an entertainment center. The period Georgia antique maintains its original "tar varnish" surface, a common finish for nineteenth-century Southern antiques.

▶ When closet space is limited, make extra storage stylish: Antique English boxes provide a decorative accent while adding stow-away space.

Mary-Kate Olsen | Ashley Olsen
MILES REDD THE BIG BOOK OF CHIC
VANITY FAIR 100 YEARS

▶ To transform streamlined furniture from "penthouse" to farmhouse, layer on an assortment of cozy throw pillows. You might even try repurposing grain sacks as pillow covers; they make perfect accessories for giving cosmopolitan pieces (like the tuxedo arm sofa separating Allison's living room and dining spaces) a little farmhouse flair.

▲ Every square foot counts in a small space, and every last nook and cranny is needed for storage (and for style). Resist ready-made (ho-hum) shelving and bins, and scout for stylish antiques, which you can creatively repurpose, instead. Allison's neatly curated bar is actually a nineteenth-century chest of drawers that fits perfectly in the unused space below the stairs. Since the spot was too low to accommodate artwork, she cleverly suspended from the ceiling the old "Grapes for Sale" sign—a vintage find that's right at home in a bar setting.

▲ If you happen upon a rental that has a unique architectural element, there's only one thing to do: Celebrate it by making it a distinctive feature in your overall room design. The blue ribbon in Allison's kitchen goes to a glass-paned service door that opens into the alleyway. In times past, furniture delivery trucks would make their way in and out of the large roll-up door (which still functions today). The sizeable doorframe would have been practical as a window or an alcove, but Allison embraced this unexpected feature and uses it to extend her living and entertaining space outdoors, to the alleyway.

▲ In an open floor plan, furnishings take center stage. And if your open-plan space doesn't have much architectural definition, you can use large furniture to define "rooms." That is just what Allison did with the help of an antique farm table. Placed just off the kitchen, it offers dining space for four and helps divide the living room from the kitchen. The table's beautifully distressed surface and original green paint also add farmhouse "bones" to the industrial architecture of the apartment.

▶ Why are open shelves such a farmhouse favorite? Because they are both practical and good-looking: They keep dishes and utensils in reach and display their everyday charm at the same time. The good news is you can get the open-shelf look with a simple bracket shelving unit from a big box store (Allison's came from IKEA). To enhance the farmhouse ambience, line the shelves with such classic country collectibles as white earthenware or copper serving pieces.

Captain John Derst's Good Old Fashioned
BREAD

Want to set a more charming and collected farm table? Try repurposing kitchen basics or salvaged items as serving pieces. Allison enlisted an old cutting board from a dilapidated baker's cabinet to do the trick. But you can take the look further with the likes of vintage soda crates, antique windowpanes, and even sections of old barnwood.

You can make an outdoor soiree on a patio, a porch, or even a back alleyway feel like a farmhouse fête with creatively chosen décor. Skimp on the likes of china and crystal, and instead set your table with a handmade tablecloth, galvanized buckets, and wildflowers, such as daisies in an enameled pitcher. Add mismatched

seating for a casual, come-as-you-are spirit. For ambience after the sun goes down, hang several strands of bistro lights to provide a festive glow.

ROSE

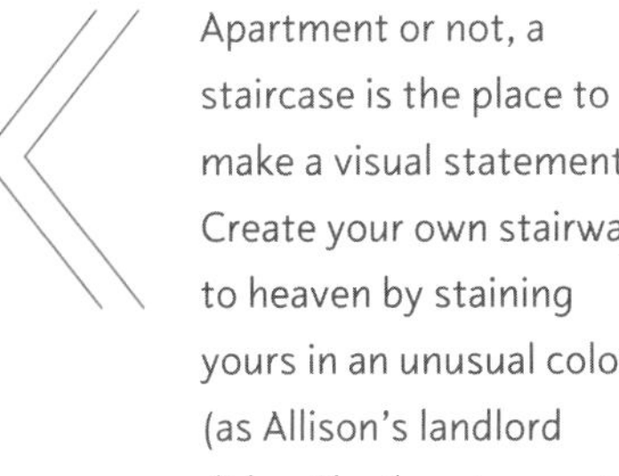

Apartment or not, a staircase is the place to make a visual statement. Create your own stairway to heaven by staining yours in an unusual color (as Allison's landlord did, with vibrant green). You can also paint a faux runner or cover the risers in wallpaper for an equally showstopping effect.

Interior doors are a smart way to change the architecture of a rental. They're easily changed—and just as easy to revert! Allison swapped the original drab, hollow-core doors of her second-floor bedroom for charming French doors, and voilà! They let more natural light into the room and make an eye-catching entrance, all without damaging the structure of the apartment.

MAKE IT FARMHOUSE STYLE

CREATE A PICTURED PAST WITH PORTRAITS

Over the years, vintage portraits of family members whose names are lost to history have found their way into all styles of decorated spaces. They ignite our imaginations with the wonderment of their untold stories, and they breathe life and history into a home, making it feel steeped in the past. This portrait trio, circa 1940s, features the same young man at different ages and adds visual interest and color to the monochromatic arrangement. For a similar look, track down a few family photos or portraits of ancestors and display them in groups.

WARM IT UP WITH RUGS

If you're missing the look and feel of weathered floors, you can easily mimic their character by using vintage area rugs. Whether your space has concrete floors, like Allison's apartment, or wall-to-wall carpeting, an area rug adds both warmth and texture. And the good news is that the more worn a rug is, the more attractive it tends to be. Look for designs with rich muted hues to give a room a farmhouse foundation. The beauty of farmhouse style is how well it accepts the mixing of periods and genres, making a home feel comfortable and conversational.

GROW A COUNTRY CONTAINER GARDEN

When apartment life is absent a green space, opt for a curated container garden instead. This compact example employs assorted discarded herb tins, an antique washtub, buckets, and baskets to pot flowering displays that are easy to tend and rotate with the seasons. The more varied your flora, the more farmhouse your container garden will appear. Nothing says country garden like a field of wildflowers, so don't be afraid to plant these spirited blooms in containers, too. For additional visual interest display a few of the containers on unexpected pieces like an antique stool or vintage country chair.

PURE COUNTRY

FOR SOME FOLKS, RENOVATING AN OLD house means updating this and modernizing that. For collectors and farmhouse-style fanatics, it often means the opposite—removing updates and going back in time to discover, and restore, a home's original character. That was Cindy Williams's dream when she stumbled upon a 1935 cottage in the historic town, and antiques hotspot, of McKinney, Texas.

It began in much the same way that many adventures do: with getting lost. She ended up on a street dotted with adorable homes and one fortuitous For Sale sign. She was taken by the classic bungalow, even though much of its interior charm had been masked by inexpensive updates. Once she bought the house and it came time to renovate, those builder-grade revisions were the first to go. Peeling back layers of sheetrock on the walls and popcorn stucco on the ceiling revealed buried treasures, including original shiplap and plank ceilings—a farmhouse enthusiast's dream come true!

Shiplap is a kind of board that has been milled with channeled edges that overlap each other to create a sturdy seal when installed. Shiplap paneling gives walls a distinctive gapped look, and a whole lot of character and dimension. Often made from rough-sawn pine or another inexpensive wood that is meant to be painted, this type of cladding is a hallmark of country construction both inside and out. Tongue-and-groove plank features an interlocking construction, with a groove on one edge and a tongue on the opposite edge. (When installed, the plank method creates a tighter seal than shiplap and is a more expensive choice.)

Since the original shiplap covered only half of the house, Cindy and her builder filled the gaps with new boards milled to match the originals. If you love this look, shiplap is now widely available and is still a great-looking, affordable option.

▲ To create a light and airy mood within a small space, go with a white-on-white scheme. Whitewashed walls, white upholstery, and collections of white accessories—like these platters and antique pitchers—will freshen the space and make it feel larger and less cluttered. The wood-plank floors and ceiling are left in a natural state to ground the white furnishings and add warmth.

◀ Transform a collection of everyday objects into a creative display, such as this artful pairing of an antique ironstone bowl and vintage shaving brushes.

▲ White canvas slipcovers and white shiplap walls provide a neutral backdrop that allows vintage pieces, such as this nineteenth-century cupboard, to shine.

▶ For a bold statement, place framed objects together in a tightly organized group. Use identical frames to keep the display cohesive.

The small sunny kitchen is chock-full of creative ideas and collections that give the space one-of-a-kind country character. In the true spirit of resourceful farmhouse style, some of the best ideas were born of necessity. When the budget didn't stretch far enough to include custom cabinetry, Cindy opted for simple sailcloth fabric instead of pricey cabinet doors and installed simple shelves instead of upper cabinets. Counters were fashioned from salvaged joists and given a proper shellacking, in a good way: with a few coats of liquid glass, also known as bar resin, to seal the wood but retain its organic beauty, knots and all. The centerpiece of the room is an island repurposed from a European prison bed that Cindy found at Bill Moore Antiques in Round Top, Texas. The piece was fitted with a plank top and a lower shelf that add both work surface and storage, not to mention a hint of cool industrial style.

BISCUITS
CAKES

▼ The niche created by a brick flue is put to good use: Cindy had a salvaged-wood spice rack custom made to fit the spot. She ordered small apothecary jars online and made her own labels to avoid the visual clutter of commercial packaging.

White porcelain measuring spoons make a collection that is beautiful *and* practical: Cooks can switch ingredients and measure happily, without having to wash spoons. Here, vintage beer steins hold the display.

◀ For instant country kitchen style, add a farmhouse sink. Vintage ones can be found at most salvage yards, and reproduction sinks are readily available, too. This authentic antique sink is installed beneath a salvaged French farmhouse window (turned on the horizontal and reframed to fit the opening).

▲ In a kitchen corner, exposed chimney bricks become a rustic backdrop for a collection of marble and wooden cake stands. Although the old, unused flue takes up space, Cindy kept it in the renovation to reflect the home's original character.

BISCUITS
CAKES

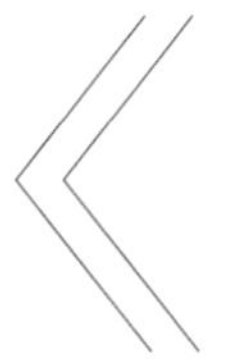

When collectibles are out of sight, they are often out of mind, so try open shelving (in true farmhouse fashion) instead of cavernous cupboards. In Cindy's kitchen, the collections are both decorative and utilitarian.

SERVE UP NOSTALGIA WITH PUNCHBOWLS

THE PUNCH BOWL HAS BEEN the center of social occasions for centuries. In colonial times, the design, the materials, and even the size of the bowl indicated social status. Typically paired with a long-handled ladle, early versions were mostly ceramic or silver. Later, manufactured molded glass versions made this serving vessel affordable to all. Now mid-nineteenth-century ironstone punch bowls are the collecting sweet spot for those who love farmhouse style. Marked by clean, classic lines, these bowls (and dinnerware) were made in simple shapes by design: British potters created white-glazed ironstone specifically to appeal to the no-frills aesthetic of rural folk. Punch bowls went by the wayside with the invention of machine-made ice that would fit into individual glasses, ushering in the era of the cocktail. They bounced back into vogue in the 1930s, with mass-produced glass punchbowls, and stayed there through the 1960s. Now we are a little punch drunk again, with these drink basins making a big comeback at wedding receptions, in social gatherings, and, especially, as collectibles.

◀ Install a transom near the ceiling to add more light to a small room or hallway. In place of a traditional window, scout for creative options like this antique sidelight. Although it once stood vertically to flank an entry door, the window offers a fresh view when installed horizontally.

▲ Once used to hold kitchen necessities in an early American farmhouse, this antique cupboard (still wearing its original blue paint) has taken on new life as storage for stacks of tablecloths, and bed linens.

▲ No early-nineteenth-century farmhouse would have been complete without a peg rail. With closet space at a premium, the minimalist rack was a necessity for coats and bulky clothing. Today, the old-style racks are prized for the same reason they were a hundred years ago: their function.

▶ A newly added bathroom borrowed space from the master bedroom. To give the small room more dimension and storage space, the architect made the wall a few feet short of ceiling height. Cindy made the fabric headboard by covering plywood with batting and natural linen.

Charmed by the original paint and simple carvings of this three-drawer cottage dresser, Cindy lugged it home from the Round Top Antiques Fair—a mecca for vintage farmhouse furnishings. The lamp was upcycled from a salvaged column and adds an interesting design element to the room.

A candlestick lamp and vintage mint julep cup make a pretty pair thanks to the silver-plated finish they share. An old, painted tin box adds a splash of color to the mostly white and natural room.

Small farmhouse rooms often have precious little wall space for a headboard. Instead of wedging one in and blocking out natural light, use the whole window as a clever alternative.

MAKE IT FARMHOUSE STYLE

CHARMING DIY CUPBOARD ENCLOSURES

Country folk typically use gathered or shirred fabric for cupboard coverings, but Cindy preferred a tailored look. She made hers by sewing buttonholes along the top edge of a fabric panel so that it would slip easily over simple cup hooks.

SWEET STYLE: DUNDEE JARS

Don't hide that pretty silverware away in a drawer. Instead display it openly and close at hand in small stoneware vessels, like antique Dundee jars.

Created by the Keiller family of Dundee, Scotland, in 1797, stoneware Dundee jars held the first commercial brand of orange marmalade simply by way of a fluke. Legend has it that the company needed to make use of a rapidly ripening shipment of Seville oranges, and rather than toss the fruit they decided to make it into a sweet preserve spread. Early examples of the stoneware jars will show their age through crackling; later models feature the telltale threads of a screw-on lid. The jars are highly sought after today for use in home décor, especially among farmhouse-style enthusiasts.

HIDE IT BARN-STYLE

When limited space doesn't allow for swinging doors, borrow an idea that was born in a barn: Suspend old four-panel doors on a sliding track. These repurposed antique doors neatly tuck away Cindy's home office and crafting space.

MADE FROM SCRATCH

THIS HISTORIC-WAREHOUSE-TURNED-LOFT- apartment in downtown Waco once housed a wholesale grocery business that serviced the small towns just south of Dallas. The soaring fourteen-foot ceilings, expansive windows, concrete floors, exposed pipes, and brick walls held not even a slight resemblance to a farmhouse. Yet for Martha and Bryan Thomas, the idea of putting a farmhouse spin on the 1,300-square-foot loft seemed like a fun and interesting challenge.

If you find yourself living in a space lacking in farmhouse charm and character, but longing to live the dream of a "down on the farm" atmosphere, don't be discouraged. Even a lofty dwelling can be an opportunity to let your creative genius shine!

To ease the transition from loft to farmhouse haven, follow Martha's lead and embrace the bones. Think of your loft as a ready canvas and design-scape-come-true for thrifted or salvaged finds. Nothing accepts castoffs more readily than weathered walls and floors, which means your scrap pile is about to achieve a whole new level of sophistication.

Hunt and gather old furnishings, vintage books, and anything hand-me-down. Get creative with vintage barn and shop cupboards (if you can find them, they can be particularly budget-friendly). This is also the opportunity to display old farm implements and parts and to use traditional farmhouse pieces in unexpected places: Use a small kitchen cupboard as a bedroom nightstand, or repurpose old tool chests as stacked storage. Once you've collected the building blocks, you'll feel much more confident about making the transformation a reality.

◀ If you have the luxury of beamed ceilings, add a bit of whimsy (and a whole lot of farmhouse charm) by suspending a wood-plank rope swing. The childhood perch will not only inspire spirited conversation but also provide extra seating—a bonus in a small space.

SALVAGED ART

WHEN A LARGE WALL calls for a thrifty art installation, gather up discarded boards, such as old ripped-away door trim and baseboards in varying shades of faded and worn paint. Martha dug through roadside trash piles and junk shops to salvage enough to create the ten-foot handmade art piece that hangs as a focal point in her family room. For inspiration on how to breathe new life into a pile of rubble, Martha turned to her always-accommodating friend, Pinterest, for advice. Here she found plenty of ideas for repurposing salvaged wood, although most pieces were on a much smaller scale. With her creative ingenuity, she was determined to create a work of art from her stash. To get just the right mix of colors and sizes, she directed the placement of each scrap while a handyman nailed the pieces in place. To finish the look, she added a green thrift store mirror (which ties in to other green accents in the room).

Old books are a staple of any farmhouse décor. Look for well-worn spines and covers and, better still, old volumes that have a unique connection to the history of the area. Here, a ledger once used at a local hardware store adds texture and interest to the room.

Small spaces often leave little room for tasks beyond the essential. Yet with a little imagination, you can carve out the perfect home office, even if all you have is a little wall space. Choose a small piece of furniture to serve as a desk and accessorize it with collectibles, globes, books, old lock boxes, even crayons in a jar. Fit a salvaged door (or an architectural fragment) with hooks and hang it above your workspace to serve as both art installation and storage rack.

STYLED
THE NEW BOHEMIANS

◀ Don't forgo creating "wished-for spots" simply because you live in a small space. Design multifunctional areas, such as a library that doubles as a dining space.

Here a seamless mix of old and new showcases a layered look in the tiny book depository. To make plain bookcases interesting, display a vintage banner or textile, like the Texas state flag that hangs here. For Martha, the old flag holds special meaning: It was a gift from her mother, a schoolteacher who once proudly displayed the flag in her classroom.

Just above the flag, a windmill remnant and a discarded water pump handle (salvaged from a farm) offer large-scale focal points that pay homage to the loft's manufacturing roots.

▶ Rounding out the space is a thrift store farm table paired with antique chairs. The colorful rug is a dead ringer for a hand-hooked, nineteenth-century floor covering, but it is actually a contemporary lookalike scored during a Cyber Monday sale.

▲ For a budget-friendly farmhouse vibe, accent your space with a bevy of salvaged finds. Martha upped the country ante in her kitchen with large, chipped windowpanes installed above the cabinets. The kitchen panes mimic the original windows that are across the way, in the loft's family room.

You can save the cost of buying a kitchen island by making one of your own out of castoffs. Martha scored big on this thrift store workbench, which she repurposed as a striking prep station. A fresh coat of white paint, a varnished top, and new steel casters made the junk piece look like new.

In a moment of country ingenuity, a vintage ladder creates vertical storage in the compact cooking space. Similarly, the striking Farmer's Market sign serves as a makeshift backsplash. While most farmhouse enthusiasts reach for the white paint when freshening up their kitchen cabinets, you can make a cheery departure by using color. A coat of apple green paint on the builder-grade cabinets adds a fresh, organic element to the industrial loft.

▶ If you're a lifelong collector and live in a small space, you have to use every nook and cranny. Case in point, this wooden display cabinet is tucked into an awkward recess for ductwork. The perfectly sized piece was once a mail sorter in an early-twentieth-century post office. Today, it has a new life as an entryway display housing a collection of thrift store milk glass. Just above, a miscellany of wood scraps creates even more stylish storage.

Färmhouse:
(farm'hous)n.,
1. a dwelling on a
POST

THE ALLURE OF VELVET

YOU MAY BE SURPRISED to know that velvet has been a part of farmhouse décor for centuries. Forever associated with the drapes and upholstery of the well-heeled (especially in the courting parlor), velvet was also beloved by thrifty farm folk. Bargain-hunted and hand-me-down fabric was proudly draped on windows, patchworked into quilts, made into luxurious bedspreads, or used as a lavish upholstery treatment for chairs and settees. Vintage pieces in both excellent and worn condition are sought after today for use in similar ways.

▲ Repurposing is synonymous with farmhouse style, and the more unexpected, the better. Mix art and candlelight by transforming vintage card-catalog drawers into unique sconces. Simply attach the drawers to the wall; then position the drawer slides to accommodate varying candle heights.

▶ Add just the right farmhouse accent to a bedroom by replacing a bedside table with an old-time kitchen cupboard. Look for a small one with glass doors so you can store (and show off) a collection of old books for handy bedside reading.

HOTE

Opposite the bed, this Danish teak dresser proves that you can fabricate a farmhouse environment no matter where you start. Crisp white chalk paint and light, all-over distressing transformed the mid-century modern gem (passed on to Martha by her mother) into a country jewel. To add to the rustic look, Martha hung salvaged shiplap planks above for a rough-hewn display shelf.

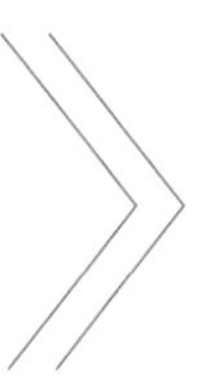

A formal gallery arrangement isn't the only way to display family photos. For a simpler, done-in-an-instant look, tack childhood vacation photos to an interesting backdrop, such as the shiplap shelving here. Arranged alongside a few inspiring quotes, they make a cheerful vignette that can be changed on a whim.

STILL
LAUGHING
WE WERE HERE
BEST DAY EVER

MAKE IT FARMHOUSE STYLE

DON'T TOSS IT! STYLE IT!

SOFAS

Think an overstuffed faux-leather sectional sofa is incompatible with farmhouse style? Before you give it the boot, try using pillows and rugs to transform the look. Custom pillows in bold patterns and colors draw the eye to their attractive design making the not so farmhouse sofa seem less obvious.

SHEEPSKIN

When in doubt, go light. White pillows and an ivory sheepskin rug provide the perfect backdrop for classic farmhouse style and blend seemlessly with the neutral tones in the room, making the sofa less of a focal point.

ROOTED IN THE PAST

FARMHOUSE STYLE IS AS MUCH ABOUT A way of living as it is about the design elements that make up a space. Lifestyle expert and host of the Design Network's *Living Big in Under 1,000 Sq. Ft.*, Theodore Leaf, and *Rolling Stone* magazine's digital guru, Matthew Habib, prove the rule with a home that satisfies their design aesthetic while connecting them with family tradition and hometown roots—a place where canning, cooking, and gardening are a way of life.

Situated in a famed hippie-chic neighborhood, in the Hollywood Hills, the tiny 800-square-foot 1940s cottage is just a seven-minute drive from Sunset Strip. Undaunted by the modern homes of their neighbors, Theodore and Matthew set out to create an updated nest that seamlessly combines antiques scored from their favorite junkin' haunts with contemporary furnishings.

The all-white interior walls make the house appear larger than it really is and offer a clean backdrop for carefully curated furnishings to command the stage. The house is abundant with large windows that enhance the airy feel of the space and swing open to a stunning view of the trees and the canyon below.

Scale and placement are much more important in a small space, and furnishings require careful consideration, since each piece becomes a focal point.

Theodore and Matthew's compact living room meets the challenge with both character and comfort. Every item is intriguing and conversational, from a classic Chesterfield sofa to a coffee table upcycled from a chain once used on the Staten Island Ferry.

apartment therapy's
BIG BOOK OF SMALL, COOL SPACES

LOUIS VUITTON
US MAIL

WHAT IS A DUTCH DOOR?

AS THE NAME SUGGESTS

Dutch doors got their start in Holland, but they were made for farmhouse living. The doors allowed fresh air to enter but not the barnyard critters that might be milling about. Doors such as these can be found at salvage and antique shops. Or, if you are handy with the table saw, you can create one by slicing a standard door in two.

◀ Small spaces in particular lend themselves to charming little features that give you that warm-and-fuzzy, storybook vibe. To make a great first impression, look for an interesting front door, like the one here. The Dutch door is original to the house and features a paneled design that hints at the inspiration for its design: the barn door.

▲ Small, well-worn cupboards are the perfect compact storage, with lots of classic farmhouse appeal, and they fit easily into tight spaces like entryways. It is interesting to note that traditional farmhouses were often short on both storage and space. Cupboards such as these were in high demand, and many were handcrafted prior to the turn of the century (making them easy to find in today's marketplace). To make the cupboard more hardworking, Theodore added hooks on either side (the canvas bag holds dog leashes; the brass mail bag stashes snail mail).

COOKING WITH COPPER

COPPER COOKWARE IS A FARMHOUSE kitchen staple, and it has been that way for centuries. It is still the choice for serious cooks, thanks to its ability to conduct heat quickly and evenly. Early copper pieces will feature telltale marks of hand hammering; later pieces were rolled smooth by machines. And though the mottled, verdigris finish is prized by some decorators, Theodore prefers it polished to new penny brilliance. He uses Copperbrill and Bar Keepers Friend, applied with plenty of elbow grease.

◀ A former chef, Theodore wanted to carve a professional working kitchen out of a pint-size space. One rule of the culinary trade is that it's critical to keep everything in sight and close at hand. So Theodore borrowed a design idea from commercial kitchens and installed a rail system for suspending his copper cookware.

◀ Once a farmhouse staple, stoneware crocks can be found throughout the kitchen. But these aren't just for decoration: Theodore uses his for making and canning his small-batch sauerkraut. His method is simple just like back in the day, when farm-to-table wasn't a culinary movement, it was the most commom way of American life.

▶ Modern kitchen and living areas are often open-plan, so it's important to keep things tidy and in tune. Open shelving in particular can quickly turn into a visual mishmash. In Theodore's kitchen, the art of display and a consistent color palette creates a cool, calm, and collected setting. Stainless cooking utensils marry (art) form and function below the open shelving. For convenience, Theodore chose clear glass containers to house cooking staples. White ironstone dinnerware and country crocks—two farmhouse favorites—warm the white kitchen without the clutter of color and pattern.

FLOUR
JENN-AIR

Southern California
UNITED AIR LINES

◀ A round table conserves space in a small eating area and creates a more convivial dining experience. Like the rest of the house, this corner is designed with simplicity in mind. Clean-lined modern leather chairs pair easily with smart built-in bench seating. Don't wait for a special occasion to get out the tablecloth. To set a pretty table at every meal, choose fabric remnants over expensive tablecloths. When they get dirty, simply throw them in the wash with the dishtowels. Theodore picked up this slice of classic toile at a fabric shop for just three dollars.

▲ To squeeze more seating into a small space, tuck a built-in bench into a corner and hinge the seats to create storage wells; this is especially perfect for old houses that lack closet space. Theodore and his grandmother made the bench cushion and throw pillows, personalizing two of them with monograms. Celebrate where you live (your hometown, too) in style by looking for vintage advertising posters with a regional theme. The old United Airlines ad couldn't be more appropriate for this California home.

▲ Theodore lends his styling talents to magazines and Hollywood industry events. Rather than a single large bouquet that takes up serving space in the center of the table—and sets up a visual roadblock between guests—he prefers individual posies tucked into drinking glasses and set beside each plate.

STRONG START: BOLD FINISH.
BIN 36

◀ The bedroom is a mere 120 square feet but the architectural details such as the tall ceilings, large transom window, beams, and mirrored storage cabinets give the room a more spacious feel. Although the space has a mostly white and neutral canvas, Theodore keeps it masculine with a leather-covered headboard, his favorite seascape, and a collection of gentlemen's suitcases.

▶ A tiny bathroom with classic farmhouse style pays homage to the dwelling's Hollywood location with Robert Abbey sconces offering star-studded light.

▼ To create a clever bedside table without taking up too much space, Theodore mounted a cleaned-up and polished nineteenth-century farm tool chest to the wall using custom iron brackets that reflect the utilitarian design of the chest.

THE FRENCH FARMHOUSE

JUST A STONE'S THROW FROM LONG ISLAND'S Jones Beach State Park and a short train ride to New York City, Debbie Fishman and Tim Meyn fell in love with a 1927 Tudor-style home on a tree-lined street in a quaint neighborhood smack in the middle of town. While most farmhouse enthusiasts would have turned away from the exterior architecture and the drab interior's dark paneled walls and outdated kitchen, Debbie and Tim saw only potential. They grabbed the chance to transform the little home into a style far removed from Long Island—a simple French farmhouse.

French country and American farmhouse make great roommates because they have so much in common. Both styles are rooted in resourcefulness and simplicity. Rarely will you find anything purely decorative in a French country home: Plates are set in wall-mounted racks (or on open shelving) for daily use, baskets corral bed linens, potted herbs add fragrance and handy flavoring for cooking.

French farmhouse rooms have an unstudied air, a naturally evolved feeling that makes the style look effortless. Family pieces mingle with favorite collections to give rooms a sense of rootedness; rustic elements mix it up with the refined. It's a personal approach that walks the line between easygoing and elegant and gives the look that laissez-faire appeal.

Debbie studied authentic French farmhouse style when she was looking for inspiration for her small Tudor-style dwelling. Through her homework she discovered hallmarks of the style that she could easily bring to her home, often with vintage American pieces. You can adapt the ideas to your rooms too; such is the easygoing nature of the *manoir français*.

In Debbie's kitchen the carefully edited and curated furnishings resemble a still life painting. To replicate this look, introduce mellow wooden accents, like French breadboards, layered with simple white ironstone. (Or, as a replacement for ironstone, contemporary everyday white dinnerware works well, too.) For additional visual interest, drop in an antique painting or a found art object. Debbie scored this period painting on the French online shopping site French Larkspur. Notice how her American farm table plays host to French park chairs; they get along beautifully thanks to the humble utilitarian roots they share.

Lighting is the key for creating an accomplished look in any space. The type of fixture that you choose will set the tone and help identify your personal style. Here, Debbie hung a vintage French work light over the farm table, but a crystal chandelier would be equally at home (if you prefer a more romantic vibe).

◀ To bring freshness and light to any room, and to set the mood for French farmhouse style in particular, rely on the favorite tool in the home decorator's toolbox: white paint. When Debbie and Tim first bought their Tudor home, it was drenched with color (and not in a good way). So they went to work with buckets of cloud-white paint. Once you have a clean slate, keep the look simple with carefully curated furniture and a thoughtfully edited mix of collectibles. Debbie's personal style mixes the old (industrial cabinets and stools) with the new (IKEA sofas scaled to fit her small space).

▲ With mostly white rooms, accessories really stand out. Think of plants as sculptural artwork. When paired with a leather book on a simple white table, these natural elements become a statement.

▼ A single showstopping piece lends character to a plain room—and keeps a streamlined interior from looking bland. With its original etched glass and graduated drawers, this old metal dental cabinet creates instant charm in Debbie's living room.

▶ Valuing all that is humble, practical, and useful is the root of both French and American farmhouse style.

Elevate your favorites by showing them off in artful vignettes. Gathered along the wall of the living room, this collection of stools resembles sculpture in a gallery. Debbie pulls the utilitarian beauties into service as side tables and extra seating when needed. Hints of soft blue add a whisper of color to the mostly white and wood interior.

miniature orchids
INTERIOR ALCHEMY
SHABBY CHIC
the comforts of home

VIKING
Mme DANEULIN
Sage-femme

◀ ▲ For a timeless kitchen, invest in iconic brands and classic materials. Rather than crowding her cooking space with superfluous things, Debbie invests in solid basics: Le Creuset enameled cast-iron cookware, marble countertops, and a Viking range—all good investments in long-term service and lasting style.

Wooden breadboards and rolling pins were once staples in both French and American farmhouse kitchens. Here, a collection of different sizes and designs becomes a sculptural art piece when displayed together.

Glass-front cupboards put kitchenware on display, add sparkle, and make any kitchen appear larger. Kitchenware is always a popular collectible, thanks to its inherent charm and sentimental appeal; who doesn't have fond memories of Grandma's kitchen? Although assembled with everyday goods, this tableau is a treat for the eyes. The centerpiece is an American-made enameled breadbox flanked by charming French café au lait bowls, breadboards, and canning jars. French Mason-style jars are a deeper green than their American counterparts.

THE FRENCH BREADBOARD: HOW TO TELL THE *VRAIS* FROM THE *FAUX*

THEY GAVE US BAGUETTES and boules, croutons and croissants. No doubt about it, the French know their bread. That's why breadboards are a staple of French country style. When hunting for a genuine one, here are some telltale signs of authenticity. First, look at the wood and the size of the board: Vintage boards are typically handmade from pine, maple, walnut, and sometimes oak and are large enough to transport multiple loaves from the oven. Some were repurposed from the tops of wine barrels and crates, and most are handmade, as evidenced by their simple shapes and rough edges. Real bread boards often have pierced handles, threaded with jute or wire loops, so they can hang on the wall. Last, check for signs of age: Worn edges (wood tends to soften around the edges as it ages), knife marks, a worn spot, slight indentations in the center of the board, and a darkened patina are all signs of the real thing.

A clever display employs pedestals and cloches to elevate the simple beauty of a small indoor garden. The wooden bases are a nod to nature; they contrast nicely with the cool marble, drawing attention to the beauty of the harvest.

Sure, you can hide your rutabagas away in the pantry, but why not enjoy their beauty as a still life while they await their turn in the stockpot? French linen dishtowels soften the edges of an American-made, blue-and-white mixing bowl in this charming centerpiece.

In her dining room, Debbie pairs a French farmhouse table with German Thonet seating and French Tolex bistro chairs. She found the folding primitive farm table in an unexpected spot: Anthropologie. Tables such as these were often used as wine tasting tables in French countryside vineyards and wineries.

Debbie continues the palette of warm white and natural wood tones into the bedroom, for a cohesive look throughout the house. Sticking to a select, neutral palette has its advantages—including making the whole space appear larger (a stylish design solution for those who love the quirky nature of old houses but not necessarily the cramped feeling of small, old-fashioned rooms).

Back in the day, when furnishings were handcrafted, attention to detail was paramount: Craftsmen routinely transformed plain boards into functional works of art. If you are fortunate enough to own such a piece, especially if it is a family heirloom like Debbie's bed, then make it the focal point of the room. When you do, you won't need to do much styling around it. Its mellowed aged surface and exquisite details will naturally draw the eye to its beauty.

▼ Who says mirrors and other displays have to hang on the wall to show off their beauty. Here, a quirky collection of insects is juxtaposed with a pair of nineteenth-century mirrors. This display is purposely unconventional, resting on a vintage French lingerie chest. The layered look gives the room coziness and character: Old silver trays, paintings, photographs, and vintage bottles would also work well in this arrangement style.

▲ Including found objects in farmhouse décor is the perfect way to tell a story or inspire conversation, particularly if the collection seems a bit out of the ordinary. Search for pieces with a single common thread, however unexpected. Don't be in a rush, since looking for pieces to add to the collection is part of the fun.

MAKE IT FARMHOUSE STYLE

IRRESISTIBLE WHITE

There's just something about white that lends itself to farmhouse décor. Its beauty shines alongside any farmhouse style—whether modern or honest-to-goodness down home country farm. Especially in simple forms, white harmonizes so well with worn finishes. Collections of white pottery and ironstone are art forms all their own, so a minimal approach is often best.

PRESERVING FARMHOUSE BLOOMS

Don't toss those flowers when their pristine blossoms fade. Dry them instead, for lasting beauty all through the year. The natural textures and soft colors of dried flowers look great in white pottery, garden pots, vases, or ironstone bowls. (Here's a tip to preserve the color of a hydrangea blossom: Keep the flower stem in water while allowing the bloom to dry out.)

EASY CENTERPIECE

To create an authentic farm-to-table mood, make fresh garden vegetables and herbs a centerpiece, just as you would a plant or flowers. Here, they take center stage on a beautiful ironstone platter.

COOL AND COLLECTED

To cut visual clutter while attractively displaying your collections, mass similar pieces together. White ironstone makes a strong but still serene statement when set against the dark wood of this simple glass-front cabinet.

STAPLE GOODS
NCLASSIFIED AND
SANFORIZED

CHAPTER 3

THE SUBURBAN CITY FARMHOUSE

There once was a time, not so many years back, when farmhouse living meant sprawling white structures surrounded by lush fields of seasonal planted crops, tractors parked in the barn, and the sounds of crickets chirping and frogs trilling in nearby ponds. (It goes without saying that city neighborhoods are the antithesis to country living.)

◄ Don't judge a home by its exterior! Today urban neighborhoods are brimming with farmhouse style and folk accessories.

Contemporary homes constructed close together in one fell swoop speak not a whisper to the style of a traditional farmhouse. Yet for those families who have chosen to decorate with this style, you'll never convince them otherwise. Look past the fresh new exteriors, the two-car garages, and the modern porches, and take a step inside—you'll be pleasantly convinced that farmhouse style lives just as passionately in the suburbs as it does on the farm. It's evidenced in the age-old furnishings, in reinvented farm pieces, in weathered mirrors and framed prints, in the lovingly restored surfaces of junk shop finds, and in the salvaged elements that turned a new build in a suburban neighborhood into a farmhouse way of living.

FRESH START

THE SPACES WE COME HOME TO ARE SO MUCH an extension of our personal and professional lives that often a life-changing event, like a new job, a marriage, or a home purchase, can make us long for a design transformation, too. There's just something about a fresh start, and letting go of the past to shift in a new direction, that is profoundly exciting. Moving into a new home is an excellent opportunity to reevaluate how your style has changed and how you want to redesign your space going forward.

Such was the goal for Andrea and Ryan Geibel when they purchased their home in a contemporary neighborhood of newly built dwellings. In their previous home, the couple's interior style was trend-driven and centered around big-brand purchases. Seeking the comfortable, laid-back vibe of farmhouse style in their new space, they devised a plan of *out with the new* (contemporary furniture and accessories) and *in with the old* (farmhouse vintage).

When going all in with a completely new look, the first step is to weed out and purge. Get rid of what you no longer want or need, and make room for seeing (and furnishing) your home in a more imaginative way. And, while purging is a necessary step on the design transformation ladder, it often brings about a not-so-exciting challenge: the budget. To keep your finances in check, adopt the mind-set that not everything needs to be completed at once. After all, the thrill of hunting and gathering those pieces that make a home uniquely yours is half the fun.

Start with a single room, perhaps the living room, and concentrate on a specific area instead of the entire space. Completing just one wall will give you a sense of accomplishment.

Consider repurposing. Perhaps something you've thought to let go can be brought back in with something as simple as a fresh coat of paint, or new hardware. Moving a piece of furniture to a different room in the house and using it in a non-traditional way can also make something suddenly seem new.

If you are in a newly constructed neighborhood, your home may have an open floor plan with the living room, dining, and kitchen all sharing the same space. These popular designs can present a real dilemma if you want to define each area. Begin by looking at each space as if it were truly a separate room. This will keep you from feeling overwhelmed as you plan. Andrea began by selecting anchor pieces, such as a sofa and rug, for the living room. Such key pieces act as a foundation that you can build upon, and they make it easier to pull in the other elements to complete the look.

Notice the pie safe (chosen for both storage and style) Andrea uses as a focal point in the living room. Once a common sight in farmhouse kitchens, this early twentieth-century example still retains its original paint. Over the pie safe, a collection of antiques adds visual interest and timeworn character.

Rugs are a key design element in any space (and the sky is the limit when choosing one that works for your home). For an interesting take on traditional floor coverings, look for hand-painted floor cloths and canvases. The rug in Andrea's living room is made from an old army tent stenciled with a graphic motif.

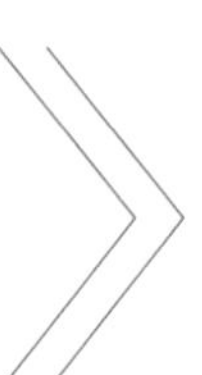

A circa-nineteenth-century, handmade child's blanket chest acts as storage—and as a resting spot, when cushioned with a homespun linen pillow from the same era. One of the beauties of farmhouse style is how well the furniture adapts to many uses throughout the house.

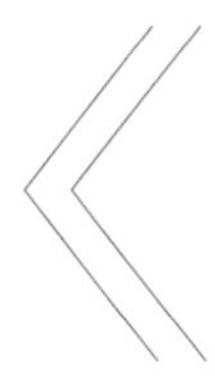

Who says repurposing can't have an edge of sophistication? This rustic-yet-elegant sofa table was crafted by repositioning the legs of a vintage stretcher to just the right height and cutting a board to make the tabletop. An artist designed the wooden stools for a compact sitting area. The nineteenth-century vintage church window now functions as a bookcase.

Old books are such a beautiful design element; their worn and tattered bindings and pages have a character that works so well in farmhouse-style interiors. So don't just stack them away on a shelf. Instead, look for a more interesting way to display them. Here, Andrea used an antique wooden furniture clamp to hold a small collection and to act as a decorative element, too. Hunt for old clamps in various sizes to create an artful effect.

MAR DE LAS ANTILLAS
Peninsula de la Guajira
Islas Sotavento
NUEVA ESPARTA
DISTRITO FEDERAL
FALCON
LARA
ZULIA
MIRANDA
SUCRE
MONAGAS
ANZOATEGUI
COJEDES
PORTUGUESA
MERIDA
BARINAS
TACHIRA
GUARICO
APURE
DELTA-AMACURO
BOLIVAR
GUAYANA
INGLESA
Georgetown
COLOMBIA
TERRITORIO
FEDERAL
AMAZONAS
BRASIL
MAPA FISICO Y POLITICO
DE LOS
ESTADOS UNIDOS DE VENEZUEL
con indicación de los productos de cada región
MAISON FOREST
E. GIRARD Geógrafo Editor, 17, Rue de Buci, PARIS
Signos convencionales
Escala

Antique books with interesting covers and bindings are design elements all their own. The collection here is the perfect scale for the bolt cabinet, and its muted colors pair well with the natural wood surface.

Bring character to a small study area with vintage accents that express a personal message. These old brass stencils were picked up at a flea market for a mere seventy-nine cents, but the sentiment is priceless!

For a pop of contrast and graphic appeal in an all-white space, display an archaic map. It doesn't have to be on a roll or framed to make a statement; simple brass tacks will do just fine and are in keeping with a more casual display in a study area.

▼ Ironstone plates and serving pieces have long been a hallmark of farmhouse décor. Nothing makes a country heart sing more than an old cupboard or rows of open shelving overflowing with this collectible dinnerware. You can step your collection up a notch by seeking old restaurant ware or pieces once given away as advertising premiums, like the one here. (Tip: For a fantastic selection, look to Fishs Eddy in New York—and online.)

▶ When a small kitchen lacks space for anything more than meal preparation, serve up some farmhouse charm by sitting a pair of stools on the opposite side of the kitchen island. It's not only an attractive design solution; it also offers a splendid hangout for family conversations (and milk and cookies).

▶ Andrea uses a primarily white color scheme and vintage textured furnishings to make the transition from the living room to the dining area in the open-plan space. Things that sparkle (like this vintage crystal chandelier) work beautifully with well-worn surfaces, old paint, and the weathered top of the farm table.

Don't take design too seriously: When seat covers get worn and soiled, simply cut a piece from a painter's drop cloth to fit the seat, with a little allowance for overhang. Next make a small slit to fit around the legs and you're ready to go with a clean new look. There's no sewing or upholstery required for this easy, budget-friendly face-lift.

◀ If you are lucky enough to have a young daughter who has an appreciation for things of the past, encourage her to take the lead when designing her private space. Young Lila blended the softness of a handmade linen bedcovering with a nineteenth-century heirloom iron bed. Since the bed is tall, she chose a handmade antique bedside table that worked with its height.

▶ Finding interesting ways to show off childhood memories without seeming too crafty is always a challenge. For a charming farmhouse look, use an old medicine cabinet to create a memory bank. Give the bank vintage character (and allow the collections to show) by scraping the silver from the back of the mirror to mimic natural wear.

The antique cabinet hanging in Lila's room is naturally timeworn. It's especially intriguing that a sweetheart's initials and a heart have been scratched by hand into the weathered surface of the mirror, giving the old piece a sentimental, storied quality.

Decorating with old books: Farmhouse stylists just can't seem to get enough. And rightly so. There are just so many ways to give them a fresh look in any design application. Lila found these sweet bound books at a shop when she was on a family trip. Displayed on her bedside table, they complement the old memory cabinet that hangs above.

HOW TO MAKE FOLDED BOOK ART

For a big impact and a budget-friendly, playful design, get DIY inspired and craft a collection of book art. These creative hangings resemble lanterns and can be folded from all different sizes of books. It's a great project to do with the kids while teaching them the beauty and resourcefulness of recycling and repurposing.

1. First, find a book with three hundred or more pages (whether paperback or hardcover, you will need to remove the cover before you begin the fold). The pattern is made by folding the pages in a series of alternating straight and triangular shapes. If your folds do not come out even at the end, remove the uneven number of pages.
2. First, fold the bottom edge of the page completely to the spine of the book, then fold the top edge of the page completely to the spine of the book to form a triangle. Fold the next page in half, and then in half again. Alternate each folding pattern until all pages are folded (as shown at middle right).
3. Once all the pages have been folded, cut a piece of jute twine to the desired length (you can braid the jute for a more interesting effect) and attach it to the center of the binding with hot glue. Fold the pages back to meet, and attach with the glue. Experiment by alternating various folding techniques and book sizes to create a varied collection.

MAKE IT FARMHOUSE STYLE

A STORIED DISPLAY

Instead of displaying a single large artwork for brief admiration, tempt passersby to linger and study intriguing arrangements: This framed collection of antique, handcrafted folk art tells the story of a vacation in 1876 to the Sea of Galilee, the Jordan River, and Athens, Greece. The nineteenth-century cut-paper urn holds a fragmented arrangement of faded blooms from an occasion not forgotten, and a handful of four-leaf clovers with a hand-drawn sentiment of "SUCCESS" offers just as much encouragement today as it did more than a century ago. Grouped with a pair of "poor man's" mirrors—the old looking-glass is backed with tin instead of mercury—the collection of souvenirs and mementos works as a story and offers a pretty design element.

WINDMILLS AS ART

Windmills have been a part of the American farming landscape since their invention by Daniel Halladay in 1854. Used primarily for pumping water and grinding grain, they are as American as apple pie, so it's not surprising that they are popular in farmhouse-style décor. A full windmill blade can span ten feet or more, so fragments are especially desirable for their decorative possibilities.

STRING POWER

Budget-friendly accent pieces, such as these old wound kite strings, look great in a farmhouse interior. They can often be scooped up for a few dollars at flea markets or in box lots at auctions, simply because most shoppers overlook their beauty and potential.

SWEET HARMONY

TODAY'S INTERIOR DESIGN IS AS MUCH about our lifestyles as it is about the decorations that adorn our homes. Nothing fits this mind-set better than the laid-back farmhouse style of living. It is a relaxed design approach that blends seamlessly with virtually any aesthetic. From traditional furnishings to flea market finds, the good news is that anything goes, as long as it soothes the senses and connects us with what matters most—a quiet place to unwind and reconnect with our family.

For multiple Grammy winner Little Big Town singer/guitarist Phillip Sweet and his lifestyle-blogger wife, Rebecca, living the dream often means spending a lot of time on the road on a tour bus. But when it's time to come home, they love settling into a space filled with the things they love most: comfortable furnishings, family pass-downs, and quirky little treasures picked up at junk and antique shops that they find in their travels. Their personal farmhouse style tells a story of rustic elegance and treasures collected along the way.

The Sweets' style is all about comfort and individuality. Their family room is a beautiful example of how well simple design, curious salvaged objects, and personal collections blend with a hint of rusticity.

The jewel of the room, and Phillip and Rebecca's favorite junkin' score, is an antique baby grand piano. The instrument was built in the 1940s by Wm. Knabe & Co. and was discovered lying on its side in a storage unit by the Nashville Piano Rescue Company. The

▲ To achieve this clean, well-edited look, choose a sofa with graceful lines upholstered in a neutral, classic fabric such as linen. With this as a foundation you can bring in rustic charm and character with ease, like the old porch table that Phillip and Rebecca repurposed as a coffee table.

story goes that in its previous life it belonged to a piano teacher back East. Beneath all the dust and grime, the original stained surface was preserved, but neglect had taken a toll on its shine. When the Sweets blew away the dust, the life of a road well-traveled was exposed and they wondered how something so beautiful wound up lost along the way. There were scratch marks and tiny flaws, but instead of removing them, they chose to honor the piano's history. To restore new life to the antique baby grand piano, the Sweets used Amish Wood Milk to moisturize the finish and Old English to camouflage scratches.

When Phillip isn't on the road touring with the band, he spends time at the old keyboard playing his favorite tunes for his family and friends.

If your home happens to present itself with quirky little features, don't shy away from them or have them removed. Instead, embrace these conversational oddities by turning them into something fun. That's what Phillip and Rebecca did with the elevator that was hidden behind a closet door in the family room. For most, hitching a ride to the cellar (renamed the basement in modern times) may seem a bit odd, but not if you're living the Sweet life. The old-school version of a modern lift mimics the swanky cars of famed historic hotels. With its paneled cherry wood walls, brass button plate, antique scissor gate, and vintage framed advertising sign, it easily makes for a conversation piece.

FOR
TEXAS
OLD WORLD
FAIR 100 YEARS
PAIN KILLER
Town

HOW WE CAME TO LOVE THE CLUB CHAIR

THE FIRST LEATHER CLUB CHAIRS WERE constructed in France around 1850. Created exclusively for gentlemen's clubs, the chairs were designed to encourage relaxed conversations among the patrons. Men would gather, have a cocktail, and smoke expensive cigars. During the early part of the twentieth century, the chairs made their way into offices, then into restaurants, and finally into home decorating styles of today. Their comfortable form and simple lines make them a favorite for farmhouse décor.

The traditional farmhouse parlor was once the only formal room in the house. It was usually furnished with Victorian or Empire seating and used exclusively for entertaining guests—and for special occasions, from weddings to funerals.

Today, it is the favored hangout for entertaining and relaxing. You can give your farmhouse parlor a modern spin with comfortable furniture and stylish accessories, like these early-twentieth-century club chairs, mirrored coffee table, vintage-inspired map, and whiskey bar. (If real-deal club chairs are not in the budget, opt for lookalikes instead.)

◀ To create the look of a gallery wall without hanging a single piece of artwork, go with bold, patterned wallpaper. This is an excellent design trick when you want to make a statement without all the clutter—or if you want to highlight a piece of furniture (as Rebecca did with a tufted velvet bed). Beneath the old farm bench she uses a dough bowl to store extra blankets, proving that farmhouse essentials can be repurposed as needed.

▶ When your home is your castle, any spot in the house can become your office. Not one to settle on a single room, Rebecca writes her popular lifestyle blog, sweetladijane, when and where the mood strikes. Dressed in layers of stonewashed linen, it is easy to see why Rebecca often uses her cozy bed as a writer's retreat.

MERCURY GLASS: IS IT REAL OR A FAKE?

ONCE REFERRED TO AS "POOR man's silver" and used as a substitute for the expensive metal, mercury glass is sought after today for its vintage appeal. With its timeworn appearance, housewares of all sorts, from lamps to candlesticks to bottles are prized by those wishing to add farmhouse flair to a space. Mass-produced pieces are now available at a fraction of the price of antiques, making mercury glass just as attractive for styling as collecting. But if you seek fine over fake, here's what to look for: It's "bottoms up" for the telltale signs of an authentic piece. Nineteenth-century production methods poured a silver-nitrate solution into and back out of the glass piece to achieve the look. This process was carried out via a small opening in the bottom of the vessel, which was later plugged and often covered with paper. Some labels and seals may be missing today, but the evidence of the silvering process will still be evident.

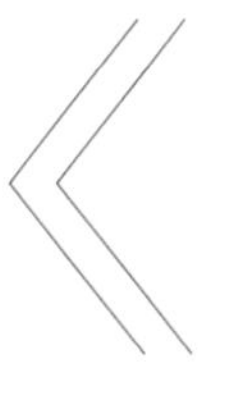

What happens when you blend a metal-inlaid farm table with overstuffed velvet chairs? You get a dining space that feels exquisitely at ease. Rebecca wanted to create a comfortable gathering area where family and friends would linger long after the meal. Traditional wooden chairs don't usually invite long conversations and storytelling, so she chose an upholstered style that blends with the rustic farm table and offers a cozy spot for swapping stories.

When you are a "story collector" like Phillip, a cracked pitcher can become a prized possession: A soldier gave him the clay vessel during the band's tour to Afghanistan. When it accidentally broke, he painstakingly glued it back together.

SETTING A FARMHOUSE TABLE

Farm tables once desired for their sturdy work surfaces are now making their way into homes as a focal point of design for a dining room or kitchen. The humble style takes many forms, from original period antiques to newly crafted reclaimed pieces. Indicative of the farmhouse style of today, table settings are just as varied as the tables themselves and feature everything from fine china and silver to rustic staples, such as Mason jars. The only rule is to draw inspiration from collections that you love.

1. Gather up mismatched plates from flea markets, or better yet, use family pass-downs. For special get-togethers, Rebecca uses an antique Royal Doulton Mandarin pattern. Her father found the dishes piled on the floor in the backroom of a retail shop. He convinced the shopkeeper that the antique plates deserved a better life, so he brought them home to Rebecca.
2. Think beyond the usual tablecloth or placemats. Consider using Turkish tea towels instead of placemats and fold the trendy cloth to allow the tassels to hang from the table.
3. Skip tradition and favor the unexpected by mixing fancy and farmhouse. Don't give a second thought to placing crystal marquis wineglasses right alongside simple Mason jars. Mix silver candlesticks and monogrammed napkins with a simple centerpiece bowl of wheatgrass and fresh pears (picked up at a local farmers' market for less than ten dollars).

MAKE IT FARMHOUSE STYLE

BLUE GLASS BALL JARS

In 1858 John Landis Mason invented and patented the molded glass jar, which he intended as nothing more than a safe means of storing food long-term. Thanks to their blend of function and stylish appeal, homemakers and decorators have crushed on the jars ever since. Whether you're a home-canning enthusiast or just like the look of the wide-mouthed vessels, the simple form is just as much a farmhouse staple today as it was over a century ago.

Collectors can estimate a jar's age based on the ever-morphing logo, but most people just like them for their bright blue glass and chalky zinc or rusty metal lids. The pieces in this collection were produced in the late 1800s through the second half of the twentieth century.

KEEP IT SIMPLE

Create a farmhouse look by keeping the focus on subtle wallpaper and understated design accents, like this salvaged nineteenth-century gilt picture frame and antique china plate. Frames make beautiful art installations and it isn't always necessary to fill them with prints or paintings. Use collections of various sizes to create an impressive showing; their hand-carved craftsmanship is often worn by the passage of time but this only adds to their charm.

PRIMITIVE PIECES

Perfect for the design challenge posed by a small corner, a diminutive, primitive table—still wearing its original blue paint—transforms a quiet spot. The tall terra-cotta olive jar would have been much too large for the tabletop; placing it on the floor incorporates it into the design while adding graphic interest to the space.

THE DESIGNER'S FARMHOUSE

WHEN YOU'RE DREAMING OF VINTAGE farmhouse character but looking at the newly minted spaces of a suburban home, the thought of making it all come together can seem overwhelming. Not everyone embraces rustic décor, but the beauty of farmhouse style is how well it blends seamlessly with the new. Lindsay and Jamey Hines are raising a young family, so it's important that the furnishings throughout their suburban Dallas, Texas, home have not only style but also a practical element. The couple prefers a natural, neutral palette with clean lines and a mix of new, vintage-style pieces alongside quirky salvaged finds, including antique farmhouse furnishings, industrial castoffs, and rescued architectural fragments.

Accents in this space are a fascinating mix of repurposed and salvaged, like the old bucket turned firewood storage, a salvaged type tray from a vintage press, and an ever-changing mix of flea market finds. The complementary accessories create a focal point and a collected, layered look that brings a chic modern vibe to this style of farmhouse decorating.

DECORATE

ELM PARK GRO.
one cannot
think well,
love well,
sleep well,
if one has not
dined well.
-Virginia Woolf

THE ART OF DISPLAY

Before pounding a nail, Lindsay has a tried-and-true method for arranging a perfect gallery wall. Try these tips for a flawless finish.

1. Clear ample space on the floor near the wall you plan to style. You will create your arrangement here before installing it.
2. Start with the largest piece first and build around it. It's all about trial and error, so try various ideas before settling on the final look.
3. Snap a photo of each arrangement to record various options and to give you a different perspective.
4. Use proper methods for hanging: Mount heavy pieces on hangers affixed to a wall stud, or use molly bolts for attaching items to hollow drywall or plaster.

◀ The personality of a home shines through the collections families gather throughout a lifetime. Don't mask their beauty behind closed doors; instead create a living still life that can be enjoyed every day.

Mix old and new in the kitchen for an interior that looks as if it evolved over time. On the counter, new canisters have classic shapes and modern lettering. Cake stands with glass domes create an eyecatching landscape of varying heights, while an old silverplated champagne bucket turned utensil corral is no longer reserved for special occassions.

Antique seating isn't always practical in a lively household. Instead, opt for stylish new versions that blend well with a vintage farmtable. Mixing textures, colors, and styles adds visual interest, too: Here, the gunmetal surface of an industrial bench complements the natural wood of the French-inspired café chairs.

one cannot
think well,
love well,
sleep well,
if one has
dined well.

◂ If you have young children at home, introduce your love for vintage farmhouse style into their spaces. It will teach them the history of times past and a beautiful way to save the planet. One idea is to carve out a pint-size artist's studio in a corner. Use carpenter's caddies, small crates, baskets, and even old milk bottles to stow crayons, drawing pencils, brushes, and paints. (To keep her kids' supplies neatly organized, Lindsay salvaged an antique shoe rack and used repurposed drawers and boxes to stash supplies.) Use caution, though, when selecting old pieces, as not everything is suitable for small ones. For the protection of little hands (and a smooth writing surface) look for sanded and sealed vintage tables, instead of more primitive ones.

The paper chalkboard overhead is a clever makeover. When Lindsay got tired of an inexpensive IKEA print, she painted over it using chalkboard paint and added a favorite quote.

▲ The cool mix of neutrals and naturals extends to the bedrooms, where Lindsay continues her carefully curated blend of old and new pieces, giving each room one-of-a-kind character. To add architectural interest to the boxy space, she hinged together old shutters to create a headboard. (Vintage barn doors and discarded farm and garden gates would work nicely, too.) The cottage-style dresser packs in more personality and storage than a typical nightstand, a reminder not to shy away from using nontraditional pieces. When space is limited, it is often necessary to double up on both function and style. Here, a galvanized desk paired with a black Tolix chair serves as both bedside table and writing surface.

TOLIX CHAIRS

OVER THE LAST FEW YEARS, THE metal Tolix chair has become a style icon. Also known as the Marais A chair, it was designed in 1934 by French metalworker Xavier Pauchard, who is also credited with bringing the steel-galvanizing process to France. He originally developed the hard-wearing, mass-produced chair for use in factories and on ships, but French café owners also loved the chair's durability and simple chicness and have turned it into a modern classic welcomed in beaucoup modern country homes. To find the real deal, look for chairs stamped with the registered trademark from the Tolix Company, which is still in operation.

In an urban farmhouse, a small patio can be the next best thing to the classic front porch. Lindsay's outdoor living area is visible from the kitchen, so she furnished it with pieces that echo the style and color palette of the interior. Found at a discount store, the slatted weather-resistant furniture offers a modern take on the classic porch swing.

▲ Buy what you love when you see it, even if you don't know how it will fit into your home. This advice particularly applies to one-of-a-kind items like this egg-sorting table, salvaged from a chicken farm. Objects unique to rural living, particularly quirky ones, are great for outdoor farmhouse-style spaces. Lindsay uses her salvaged piece as a patio table, where it corrals a mini landscape of small plants and succulents. Swap the plants for wooden trays and the egg sorter works as a serving table—an added bonus!

▶ For a farmhouse-style container garden—the urban farmer's answer to a tilled land—galvanized buckets, tubs, and barrels are essential. Since you may need to drill drainage holes into the bottom of any container you use, choose copies and finds over real-deal antiques. Don't limit yourself to flowers; many herbs and vegetables can also be sown in containers.

MAKE IT FARMHOUSE STYLE

BASKETS AS ART

Baskets of all varieties have been a farmhouse classic for centuries, weaving together function and handmade beauty. Tobacco baskets, like the pair used here, are popular for their flat, open-weave construction—perfect for wall display. Used from the 1800s until the 1980s to display tobacco at markets, the baskets are affordable and relatively easy to find. Authentic examples are created with hand-riveted oak strips and nails that show their age.

OPT FOR NEW WHEN OLD WON'T DO

When an old cupboard isn't deep or practical enough to accommodate modern electronics, shop for a new piece that has a barn-aged look. Lindsay found this vintage-style piece at Restoration Hardware. The straightforward, stripped-down look blends easily with most interiors.

GALVANIZING GOOD LOOKS

GALVANIZED METAL was a farm staple beginning in the late 1800s, and the rust-resistant zinc finish was a game-changer for resourceful farm folks. Early pieces were constructed first, then coated with zinc. Later, metal was galvanized before it was manufactured—into everything from watering troughs to cream cans. Today, galvanized pieces are snatched up by farmhouse enthusiasts for their soft gunmetal patina and simple charm.

DEPOSIT YOUR STOWAWAYS IN A BANK OF DRAWERS

Looking over the shoulder of a clean-lined, linen-clad sofa, an old galvanized bank of drawers now organizes family photos. This one was pretty rough-looking and forlorn in the corner of an antique shop when Lindsay rescued it; she revived it by sanding, sealing, and painting over water damage. The slender construction of this once commercial piece was designed for maximizing storage with space-saving features. If industrial design isn't your forte, look for the wooden counterparts. Found in mercantile and drug stores back in the day, these multidrawer apothecaries are a favorite farmhouse-style design element.

SALVAGED STYLE

YOU'RE FINALLY BUILDING THE HOUSE OF your dreams in one of the most beautiful and desirable neighborhoods in the city. It's a thrilling time in your life! You've explored Pinterest for months, ripped pages of farmhouse-style articles from your favorite shelter magazines, and bookmarked hundreds of ideas in decorating books. The dream of creating your city farmhouse is about to come true, but deep down the spark of excitement is fizzling. You keep telling yourself a new build has so many advantages: less upkeep over the long haul, everything fresh and shiny, the paint on the walls crisp, and not so much as a scuff on the floor. It all seems so perfect, so why the Negative Nellie attitude?

What's keeping you from your joyful jubilee is the BONES! If your new house seems too "new," it's time to put the timeworn personality you love into all that is slick and shiny. You'll not only have family and friends seething with envy, but you'll be over the moon, too! The floors, the doors, the trim, the fireplace: You can easily give them all a good dose of rough-hewn charm. Thanks to the abundance of discarded building materials at architectural salvage yards, flea markets, and antique shops, creating a period style within a new construction is within your reach—and affordable, too. As a matter of fact, with the right design choices you can make your new city home feel like a true country retreat.

That is exactly the approach Lucy Farmer and her husband, Conner, took when they built their home in Birmingham, Alabama: With a design philosophy of incorporating as many salvaged materials as possible, the couple was able to create a farmhouse look in every room in the house. Central to the construction plan was reclaimed wood—lots of it. Throughout the house, salvaged wood floors provide an instant age-old aesthetic. Similarly, every door in the home is an antique, with the original patinaed surfaces and the more-than-one-hundred-year-old paint left intact, no two are alike, and each is from a different era or historic location. But the Farmers didn't stop there; moldings, smartly chosen finishes, fixtures, and found fragments were added to further enhance the character and charm.

For farmhouse-style enthusiasts, a fireplace is often *the* element that is synonymous with the character of a rural dwelling. In newly built homes, the homeowner may simply create a mantel with an antique hand-hewn beam salvaged from a barn or an older home. But instead of just warming up the new, why not go all in with the old by using salvaged finds to construct the firebox, façade, and hearth? Here Lucy used antique bricks from an old Alabama homestead and cobblestones from the rutty streets of an Ohio town at the turn of the century.

◄ Using antique exterior doors as interior ones gives a whole new meaning to bringing the outside in. But when you stop and consider that the average home has ten or more doors, you realize the potential to make a serious design statement. To preserve their individuality, Lucy kept them as she found them, with evidence of a well-served life. Notice the circa-nineteenth-century door leading to the powder room, which retains its original white paint and charming letter slot.

PRESERVING SALVAGED DOORS

If you love the patina on old doors, you can easily clean the surfaces while keeping their storied finishes intact. Techniques differ, depending on whether the door is painted or stained and varnished:

FOR PAINTED OR NATURAL WOOD DOORS

1. Whisk away loose paint with a soft bristle brush and then wet the door thoroughly using a garden hose. If the door has a build-up of grime, spray it with a household degreaser and let the degreaser work for approximately five minutes.
2. Dip the soft bristle brush into a bucket of hot soapy water (dishwashing detergent will do), scrub the surface clean, and spray off the loosened dirt and grime using the garden hose. Repeat until the door is clean. Then allow it to air dry for two days or until you can no longer feel moisture in the wood.
3. Wax the surface with a paste wax of your choice, but do not allow the paste to stand (as directed on the can). Apply the wax and buff immediately, always following the grain of the wood. Do not use a circular motion. Continue to apply coats of wax, usually a couple will do, until you achieve a smooth surface.

FOR VARNISHED DOORS

1. Whisk away loose dirt with a soft bristle brush and then submerge a clean soft cloth (an old T-shirt works well) into a solution of Murphy Oil Soap or other wood cleaner (following package directions) and wring out any excess water.
2. Wash the door with the cloth. If the grime is excessive, scrub with a soft bristle brush dipped in the solution. Repeat until the door is clean, but be careful not to oversaturate the surface with water. Rinse using a fresh cloth and warm water. Then allow the door to air dry for two days or until you can no longer feel moisture in the wood.
3. Apply lemon or orange oil to a soft cloth; do not apply directly to the wood. A spray-on version of the product works best to evenly coat the cloth. Wipe over the surface with the oiled cloth. Allow to dry and repeat until the surface achieves a warm glow.

◀ This smart juxtaposition of old and new sparks conversation: Lucy's coffee table boasts a vignette that pairs vintage periodicals (a bound volume of the 1931 editions of the *New York Times* and a 1959 personal property ledger) with an ethereal glass sculpture crafted in Normandy, France.

▼ An abundance of old-fashioned medicine bottles makes a fascinating display. Achieve a similar look by grouping old Mason jars, soda pop bottles, bud vases, or even cowbells in a rustic crate or storage box with deer antlers as unexpected handles!

▶ Unexpected furnishings and textures give the modern-day farmhouse its storied vibe: This 1930s zinc apothecary, lacking several drawers, makes what once was a southern farmer's nuts and bolts storage bin into a piece of art. Don't let missing parts, imperfections, carved initials, dents and dings dissuade you from things you love. Instead, embrace the history of long years of service and use. These are the things that infuse an old piece with soul and character. Finding the beauty in these "flaws" is essential for creating farmhouse style.

Integral to the farmhouse look is the design of layered vignettes. You can take an old piece up a notch by adding a little interest to the top. Here, a glass demijohn bottle, a vintage pulley wheel, and a bevy of candles create a striking mix.

do all
things
with
love

◀ The kitchen: the most celebrated room in the house. Not only a spot for preparing meals and dining, it's often the hub for daily planning, socializing, honoring achievements, and on occasion comforting the disappointed with a warm batch of freshly baked cookies. Next to cookies, nothing evokes comfort like the well-worn finishes of a farmhouse kitchen. Here, the range hood, crafted from a discarded piece of barn tin, tones down the shiny new stove, and reclaimed heart pine softens the custom cement top of the kitchen island. The pendant lights are an up-styled contemporary version of the farmhouse porcelain shades that were popular in the 1920s.

You can unify a multitextured look like the one in this kitchen with color: For Lucy, that meant installing hardwood floors taken from a general store in Tennessee. The reclaimed boards echo the rich hues rooted in the other finishes.

▲ Looking for a centerpiece with both farmhouse style and far more personality than a ho-hum vase? Try a weathered dough riser. Its low profile lets you display flowers and collections without obscuring the view across the table. This version, found in France, has a particularly unique design.

SCAPE

◄ ▲ Turn antique windows into true showstoppers by placing them in an unexpected spot. Lucy converted a trio of stained glass windows into one unforgettable headboard; the jewel tone hues of the six-foot-tall, circa-nineteenth-century windows, salvaged from a church in Jacksonville, Florida, create a dramatic counterpoint to the airy white walls.

AWARD

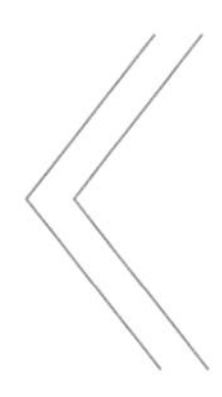

It goes without saying that good design is in the details. Don't be afraid to introduce a few dilapidated items into your design storytelling. Lucy paired this weathered black-and-white print with an exquisitely worn frame that she rescued from the rubble of a house. The decomposed elements give the wall hanging its farmhouse elegance.

In a space built around a collection of oddities, an unusual nineteenth-century window and an old wooden mold (recycled into a quirky clock face) take on new roles as folk art.

WHAT IS A YARD-LONG?

IT WAS EARLY IN THE twentieth century that panoramic photographs made their debut. Also known as "yard-long photos," owing to their approximately thirty-six-inch length, these large photographs frequently depicted cityscapes, military units, or graduating classes. Today it's relatively easy to come across one in its original frame. (Don't let cracked glass like the one next to Lucy's bed deter you; it is part of the charm!) Their sizable scale and historic subject matter create a smart, visual time capsule for any room.

With a hero piece like the stained-glass headboard, you have to be mindful of balancing the other accents in the room. Subdued accessories will do the trick, as shown here: A distressed mirror and two vintage photos (one a panoramic photograph from Harvard's Chaplain School, Class of 1943; the other Lucy's father in his navy uniform) are large enough to match the visual heft of the windows but have a monochromatic palette and squared-off design that allows the windows to remain the focal point.

Often, the thrill of the hunt ends in a unique discovery, such as these nineteenth-century exterior doors. At first glance, all that glass doesn't seem appropriate for a bathroom. The surprise is that these doors are outfitted with shutters that face the opposite side and can be closed for privacy.

◀ Cast-off fragments can become true objets d'art: Wooden hammers from a grand piano, organ keys, architectural salvage, old weathervanes, and rescued farm implements are a few examples of discards that merit artistic appreciation. The golden tones of this corrugated piece rescued from a Dumpster strikes a perfect chord with the antique oak door in Lucy's entryway.

▶ The best farmhouse rooms blend periods and genres; not everything has to look rural. A little upscale sophistication is not only acceptable but also encouraged. In this master bathroom, antique salvage steals the show with a lead crystal chandelier plucked from the demolition site of a nineteenth-century hotel in New Orleans. An ornate window from a prominent structure in Philadelphia sets the stage for dreamy relaxation in a modern-day version of a nineteenth-century soaking tub.

CHAPTER 4

THE CREATIVE CITY FARMHOUSE

While farmhouse style's utilitarian roots may seem at odds with workspaces, urban gardens, and even the office, pieces with a past inevitably encourage imagination, artistry, the telling of new stories, and the pursuit of new projects.

◀ Farmhouse style isn't just for dwellings anymore! In recent years, the look has made its way into unexpected spaces, encouraging relaxation and creativity wherever you choose to carve out a spot.

And, what could be more inspiring than surrounding yourself with a décor that speaks to your soul and offers up a relaxed environment too? What's more, these tiny getaways can be tucked in an unassuming spot. Good news is today the look is pushing boundaries in all design applications. Who says you can't grow a vegetable garden on a rooftop, or patio, or create a cozy little hideout over the garage, or even display bugs all across the wall in a tiny studio office? Maybe it's time to convert that old shed out back into a restful retreat. Take advantage of the opportunity to soak up this laid-back vibe on a small scale wherever you find a little personal or private space.

THE WRITER'S LOFT

CREATING A SANCTUARY, NO MATTER HOW tiny, to retreat from the hustle and bustle of life offers a perfect opportunity to express your own personal style, showcase collections, and encourage creative juices to flow. Such was the goal of singer-songwriter and nine-time Grammy Award–winner Sheryl Crow, when she decided to transform her garage attic into a writer's loft and a welcoming hangout and guest retreat for her fellow musician friends. Inspired by her large stockpile of antique trade signs, she gathered the most eye-catching examples to create a fun and inspirational space.

The light and airy design for the 500-square-foot loft relies on white shiplap walls (to form a canvas and properly show off her sign collection) paired with dark hardwood floors, which add depth.

Because the main room serves as a passageway to the other spaces in the loft, it was important to keep the area clutter free. Staying visually rooted in what really matters was the goal—lots of "stuff" would fight for the eye's attention and cramp the room's open style. Artful pillows and a trio of vintage string balls keep the focus on the folk art charm and personality of the space.

▲ A marshmallow-soft sofa, chairs with an open framework, and a higher-than-average coffee table contribute to the sense of spaciousness and light. Since privacy isn't an issue, the bare windows also open up the small interior (a trick you can employ anywhere, since light and a clear view to the great outdoors push back the boundaries of a room).

PIANOFORTE & MUSIC CO.
PERFECT BALANCE
SAVE HERE
TO BUILD YOUR HOME

In a mostly white space, use bold black accents as a graphic form of "eyeliner" to add definition and contrast. Sheryl is particularly drawn to old signs that have a musical, religious, or equestrian theme. For uncluttered style and visual impact, she selected large pieces that fill entire sections of wall space.

Wheels from old carnival games put a unique spin on wall art in the stairwell. Their circular shapes break up the straight lines of the shiplap, windows, and stair banister.

COLLECTING VINTAGE AND ANTIQUE SIGNS

BOTH PERIOD AND VINTAGE TRADE signs have maintained their collectible appeal for decades. Eye-catching by nature, they have great personality—and often a personal meaning to the collector. Plus, their simple graphics easily slip into many interior styles.

Steel-based signs with a porcelain coating are in high demand. Not only does their super-strong construction last for several generations, but they are usually less expensive than their wooden counterparts. However, be wary when you spot one for sale; huge numbers were recycled for metal during World War II. Authentic examples will show even wear, not just rust around the edges. More modern signs have enamel coating, so bring along a magnet to help you determine the early steel models when you shop.

Antique (meaning they've celebrated their one hundredth birthday) wooden signs are typically more expensive than the vintage steel ones. The authentic ones are always hand-painted, so look for brushstrokes and the imperfect lettering of handmade art (some may have gold leaf decoration and a more detailed artistic quality). Unlike other farmhouse collectibles, wooden signs are valued higher when in less worn condition.

NEW YORK. CHICAGO.
LONDON. PARIS.
DNER
GIL

◀ Sheryl brings her work home in all of her living spaces, but here a vintage 1964 Gibson J-200 guitar feels as much a part of the art collections as it does onstage as a musical instrument.

▶ Small bedrooms often leave few choices for arranging furniture. In a guest room with only a windowed wall for placing a bed, Sheryl chose a simple spool headboard that would support natural homespun pillows without blocking the light and the view. The effect? A pretty bank of windows and a stunning treetop view for a delightful "rise and shine"!

Next to the bed, an antique candlestick table gets the job done but takes up far less space than a nightstand would. In a small space, even minor decorating choices—such as the color of your lampshades—have a big impact. Silhouetted against the white walls, the black lampshade adds an effective contrast while directing the light where it needs to be for nighttime reading—or songwriting.

▲ A downhome girl who likes to entertain as simply as she decorates, Sheryl serves up comfort food—simple peanut butter and jelly sandwiches on vintage chopping boards. Whether cut into charming animal shapes or squares and rectangles, chopping boards are a classic; no farmhouse kitchen should be without one . . . or several!

▶ Industrial pieces like these factory stools have a strong, sculptural presence that's perfect for small spaces where you want to limit the number of furnishings. White cabinetry is an obvious choice in a small galley kitchen; however, too much of it can seem cold and a bit sterile. The black soapstone countertops break up the white and add definition to this pass-through space. Their matte finish has a quieter, more natural effect than fancier marble or granite.

Clever, upcycled furnishings are a great match for farmhouse interiors—they nod to the resourcefulness and humble materials used by country folk. The pendant light in Sheryl's kitchen is made from a wire egg basket and is a fun, functional, and easy DIY project that takes about fifteen minutes.

COFFEE SHOP

SOPHISTICATED STUDY

WHETHER IT IS AN EXTENSION OF THE workplace, a writer's studio, or a quiet space to muddle through the household budget, a home office deserves just as much style as the rest of the house. That's how Tanya Cross (an Australian interior designer turned missionary) felt when she and her husband, Matthew, returned stateside after spending much of their married life caring for orphans and rebuilding hospitals in Third World countries. Seeking a comfortable home for her family, Tanya drew on her love of the humble spirit of the rural farmhouse—yet the lavish interiors of the multimillion-dollar homes she once styled as a residential designer kept coming into play.

One habit she would never break was decorating with curated oddities. Nature is the inspiration for much home décor, and insect-inspired collections remain at the forefront. To create a dramatic and striking display, Tanya repeated the image of a Christmas beetle across the large wall of her study. The prints are actually images cut from wallpaper and mounted in barnwood frames from a hobby store.

If, like Tanya, a sophisticated farmhouse is more your mind-set, you can strike a balance between the two by lending a touch of elegance to farmhouse essentials. While vintage and antique pieces are often the backbone of the look, a modern and contemporary version can be just as appealing.

In barns, in workshops, and sometimes sprawled on the lawn, the simplest work surface ever invented was born from a loose board rested on a pair of humble trestle legs. The material for the top could be anything on hand: a discarded door, a scaffolding board, or a mere piece of plywood. Nothing was ruled out as long as it filled the need. These bases were, and still are, called sawhorses, and as the name implies, they were built for use in construction.

Today, thrifty farmhouse-style enthusiasts assemble a similar version as an office desk, work surface, or even for dining. But if DIY is a bit too primitive for your taste, look for readymade versions and spruced-up reinventions of the old makeshift table.

SELECTING THE PERFECT LAMPSHADE

NOTHING ADDS MORE STYLE TO a room than the perfect lampshade, but selecting one with the proper look (and fit) can be a challenge. Take the guesswork out of the process with these foolproof steps: First, define your aesthetic. Is your lamp base and room more farmhouse rustic or farmhouse refined? Drum shades work in both county and modern décor, while pleated and bell shades are more traditional. Next, consider the fabric. Natural linen is always an excellent choice for any décor. If you're on a budget, opt for a linen-look paper shade. Also, consider how much light you'll need. The denser the material, the less light the shade will provide. Be sure to measure for size. As a general rule, the shade should be a third to half the height of the base. The size of the table that the lamp is displayed on will dictate the shade's diameter. Last, pay attention to the details. A shade should be tall enough to cover the harp, and the lamp should always be crowned with a finial. Shades with a bit of personality, like the cut-and-pierced one here, echo the old handcrafted tin and copper versions from the early twentieth century. You can hand-punch your own to get the look or buy manufactured paper die-cut versions.

▶ In keeping with her upscale-farmhouse vibe, Tanya uses a credenza in place of a bookshelf. A taxidermy mount of an Australian deer, brought along from her homeland, is a prized possession and unique focal point, and the fragment of architectural salvage makes an impressive accessory. Decorating with insects and mounted animal heads isn't anything new. The Victorians proudly displayed their insect collections and prized taxidermy trophies as art, giving them prominent positions in parlors all across America and England. Insects were hand-painted on porcelain tea service sets and dinnerware, while collected specimens were encased in paperweights. In the late nineteenth century a style known as anthropomorphic taxidermy became popular; it featured mounted animals cast as people or engaged in human activities.

◀ Tanya's personal taste leans more toward refined charm, so she stepped it up with a manufactured chrome-and-glass version of the old sawhorse table, proving that it doesn't have to be handmade and well-worn to be farmhouse. All that's necessary is that it speaks to your soul and satisfies your design aesthetic.

TOP-OF-THE-TOWN GARDEN

IT'S ALMOST IMPOSSIBLE TO IMAGINE farmhouse-style living without picturing a back porch. It is the place where stories are told, sweet tea is sipped, and laughter is the most prominent form of conversation. Whether you have a patio in the suburbs or a small balcony in the heart of the city, with the right mix of recycled furniture, salvaged architectural finds, and old farm castoffs you can easily turn urban porch sitting into a farmhouse state of mind.

That's just what Kimberly Kelly did with her rooftop deck in historic downtown Franklin, Tennessee. The artist and designer even added container gardens for a true backyard atmosphere and a bountiful harvest of vegetables and herbs throughout the seasons.

To create an outdoor space with a down-home feel, look past straight-from-the-box outdoor furniture and head on out to a nearby flea market instead. For a back porch with true farmhouse flavor, you'll want weatherworn, vintage seating and tables that look and feel authentic. You can freshen up worn-out cushions with an impromptu cover by simply wrapping the seats with a painter's drop cloth—that's what country folks would do. While most farmhouse interiors shy away from bold accessories, here is your chance to go bright and cheery. Gather a bevy of throw pillows in various textures and colorful patterns for genuine "use what's on hand" character.

CRESCENT ST
BEHRENS

◀ A back porch is all about family and friends conversing around a table of deliciously prepared home-cooked dishes. If your outdoor space allows for alfresco dining, then a farm table should be your gathering spot. To ensure yours is up to braving the elements, follow Kimberly's lead and seek out one made from pressure-treated lumber or build your own in vintage style just as Kimberly did. Her painted piece has weathered the outdoors for nearly ten years. Just to prove that farmhouse style mixes well with almost anything, Kimberly paired the table with mid-century iron garden chairs and a geometric indoor/outdoor rug.

▲ Almost anything can become a work of art if it speaks to the soul. The very essence of farmhouse style is finding the beauty in the lost, the found, the abandoned, and the forgotten. An old plaster-of-Paris compote takes on new life when filled with broken china. Nineteenth-century Delft plate fragments, along with a scrap of a shepherd boy figurine, lie among bits and pieces of the unrecognizable. The patterns and textures intermingle in a poetic abstract work and form a decorative display from what could have been tossed away.

▲ Instead of traditional paired candlesticks, set the mood for relaxing with a candlelight tableau. For an even more casual look, arrange wax pillars of various heights on a marble remnant. The marble makes for a sturdy, organic, and wonderfully reflective base.

▲ Even the smallest and most urban garden can take on a farmhouse aura, thanks to salvaged containers straight from the farm. Look for buckets, horse troughs, washtubs, trashcans: Most anything galvanized or aluminum will do. This compact green space supports flowers, ornamental trees, fruits, and vegetables. Kimberly has created a mini farm-to-table movement right on her rooftop, with farm favorite veggies and herbs.

◀ Farmhouse décor frequently brings the outside in. So why not mix it up a bit and bring the inside out! Kimberly wanted to infuse her rustic rooftop with some sophisticated elements, so she added paintings and busts (usually reserved for formal interiors) as decorative features. Similarly, the chipped mantel (moved from Kimberly's former farmhouse) adds lived-in style that's brimming with country charm. If you're short on space, you can achieve a similar look with smaller-scale salvage, such as corbels or window frames.

◀ Birdbaths come in all shapes and sizes and their shallow bowls make a prime spot for growing herbs. Kimberly grows thyme, which is relatively maintenance free, in this seahorse yard ornament.

CHAPTER 5

PICKIN' PLACES

RESOURCES FOR CREATING CITY FARMHOUSE STYLE

If over the river and through the woods to Grandmother's house won't get you the kind of farmhouse style that you're looking for, then here are some prized pickin' spots that are guaranteed not to disappoint.

◀ There is no better feeling than scoring a special piece that works perfectly in your home or creative space.

Many of these tried-and-true haunts have been our mainstays for the last twenty-four years, delivering up unique furnishings and curious oddities for farmhouse-style enthusiasts, interior designers, and commercial clients who look to our retail store to supply their farmhouse-style needs. On any given adventure we've never turned up empty-handed, and on multiple occasions we've bought more than we could haul, making for several long-distance trips back and forth from pickin' spot to home to get it all there. We hope that these honey holes will get you on your way!

RESOURCES

ALABAMA

THE MARKET AT CHAPEL HILL
The Waters
24 Ring Around Road
Pike Road, Alabama 36064
thechapelatthewaters.com
205-296-9757
October annually
This quaint little annual market brings together popular home-decorating bloggers and curated farmhouse-style vendors to the tiny town of Pike Road, Alabama. Though the market is small, it's big on farmhouse-style antique and vintage home furnishings.

VINTAGE PICKIN' BARN SALE
202 Farmer Road
Fyffe, Alabama 35991
vintagepickin.com
256-717-9365
Spring and fall
This open-air shopping event on a family farm brings together vendors offering vintage and antique furnishings. You'll likely pick up an antique farm table here.

SOUTHERN ACCENTS ARCHITECTURAL ANTIQUES
308 2nd Ave SE
Cullman, Alabama 35055
sa1969.com
256-737-0554
If architectural salvage is what you are looking for, whether it's for restoration or simply for decoration, you will find it here. This family-owned business has been around forever, and it's likely the largest salvage house in the southeast.

CALIFORNIA

JUNK BONANZA SAN DIEGO
Del Mar Fairgrounds
2260 Jimmy Durante Boulevard
Del Mar, California 92014
junkbonanza.com
Every February, Ki Nassauer, editor in chief of *Flea Market Style* magazine, plays host to more than two hundred vendors offering everything from farmhouse style to mid-century modern.

REMNANTS OF THE PAST ANTIQUE SHOW
Earl Warren Showgrounds
3400 Calle Real
Santa Barbara, California 93105
remnantsofthepast.com
For authentic farmhouse style, this is one show you don't want to miss. Held annually in November, you will find everything farmhouse from décor to folk art.

THE ROSE BOWL FLEA MARKET
101 Rose Bowl Drive
Pasadena, California 91103
rgcshows.com
323-560-7469
Second Sunday each month
This famed Southern California flea often attracts the rich and famous as well as designers from all over the world. With more than 2,500 vendors, it goes without saying that it's a great place to shop!

TUMBLEWEED & DANDELION

1502 Abbot Kinney Boulevard
Venice, California 90291
310-450-4310
tumbleweedanddandelion.com
Lizzy McGraw has been creating custom home furnishings since 1997! But that's not all you'll find in this beautiful Venice shop, just blocks from the beach. Lizzy has an eye for antiques and vintage of a folk art and curious nature. Her home is amazing—you may have seen it in *This Old House* magazine.

COLORADO

OLD GLORY ANTIQUES

1930 S. Broadway
Denver, Colorado 80210
oldglorystyle.com
303-798-4212
This amazing shop combines the age-old past with furnishings of today that blend seamlessly together. Twice a year the proprietor hits the road to Round Top, Texas, to take part in the famed Antiques Week. The occasional shop is filled with goods that you'll find at the Denver location.

FLORIDA

RENNINGERS FLEA MARKET

20651 U.S. Highway 441
Mount Dora, Florida 32726
renningers.net
352-383-8393
January, February, November annually
This huge open-air market is known for vintage and antiques. It's a must for architectural and garden finds.

GEORGIA

COUNTRY LIVING FAIR

Stone Mountain National Park
Stone Mountain, Georgia 38007
stellashows.com
866-500-fair
October annually
Hosted by the popular shelter magazine of the same name, the Stone Mountain show is the fourth of four *Country Living* fair annual events. It's where the pages of the magazine come to life. So of course you must go!

LOUISIANA

RUSTY ROOSTER

211 N Range Avenue
Denham Springs, Louisiana 70726
rustyroosterllc.com
225-667-1710
This shop is a must stop on the hunt-and-gather trail. Julie and Chad exhibit at our pop-up fairs, and they never fail to deliver the absolute best in architectural and vintage farmhouse style, plus the other oddities that they seem to find on their pickin' jaunts. I once bought a pair of amazing nineteenth-century boudoir mannequins from the couple.

MARYLAND

DIXON'S AUCTION

2021 Dudley Corners Road
Crumpton, Maryland 21628
crumptonauctions.com
410-928-3006
Every Wednesday at 9 a.m. sharp
For a true auction experience like no other, this is the place to be. Two large, open fields and an enclosed

auction barn set the stage for the selling of everything from junk to period antiques. You'll have to be quick with the bidding though. The three auctioneers waste no time in moving anywhere between three thousand and six thousand lots by 5 PM the same day! Not only will you find fabulous vintage and antique pieces, but this auction is also loads of fun!

MASSACHUSETTS

BRIMFIELD ANTIQUE SHOW

35 Palmer Road
Brimfield, Massachusetts
brimfieldshow.org
May, July, September annually
Three times a year the tiny town of Brimfield, Massachusetts, plays host to what has become the largest outdoor antiques and collectibles show in the northeast. This six-day event takes place in twenty-one fields along an extended stretch of Route 20 and attracts more than five thousand vendors (I think that's being modest)! You will literally find everything you need to furnish your home in farmhouse style in a one-stop shopping trip—that is, if you bring a large enough vehicle and bankroll!

MINNESOTA

JUNK BONANZA MINNEAPOLIS

Canterbury Park
1100 Canterbury Rd S.
Shakoppe, Minnesota 55379
junkbonanza.com
April and September annually
Once again, Ki Nassauer, editor in chief of *Flea Market Style* magazine, plays host to more than two hundred vendors offering everything from farmhouse style to mid-century modern, vintage, and antique finds.

MISSOURI

HISTORIC WEST BOTTOMS, KC

Kansas City, Missouri
kcwestbottoms.com
Monthly
The historic West Bottoms of Kansas City is a repurposing story within itself. The site was once the hub of manufacturing and distribution along the Missouri River, but flooding from the river and economic hardship took its toll. That's when a group of antique dealers stepped in and upcycled the old buildings into a pickin' mecca. There are eighteen-plus shops to get your junkin' on, but my favorites for farmhouse style are Top Hat Mercantile, Bella Patina, Stuffology, Bottoms Up Antique Market (floor after floor), and Hello Sailor.

ARTICHOKE ANNIE'S ANTIQUE MALL

1781 Lindberg Drive
Columbia, Missouri 65201
573-474-2056
It's not often that you'll find a large antique mall filled with 99 percent antiques and vintage. Here, you will. It's proven that you can fill a trailer—that's speaking from experience!

VINTAGE MARKET DAYS OF ST. LOUIS

16365 Lydia Hill Lane
Chesterfield, Missouri 63017
vintagemarketdays.com
918-850-8544
This is an amazing upscale farmhouse-style market! If architectural salvage is your forte, then this is the place to shop.

NEW YORK

WHITE FLOWER FARMHOUSE

53995 Main Road
Southold, New York 11971
instagram.com/whiteflowerfarmhouse
631-765-2353
Yes, it's white and natural farmhouse all the way! Ironstone, cupboards, tables, and more! The best in the area!

COUNTRY LIVING FAIR

Dutchess County Fair Grounds
6550 Spring Brook Avenue
Rhinebeck, New York 12572
stellashows.com
June annually
Hosted by the popular shelter magazine of the same name, this is the second of four amazing fairs featuring more than two hundred vendors offering our favorite—farmhouse style!

FISHS EDDY

889 Broadway
New York, New York 10003
212-420-9020
fishseddy.com
It's the place to go for oddities, but most important this NYC store houses the world's largest collection of restaurant ware!

ABC CARPET AND HOME

888 Broadway New York, New York 10003
212-473-3000
abchome.com
I have an ongoing love affair with everything in this store. Like no other, the in-store designers have the ability to combine farmhouse with many other styles; their displays will give you the inspiration to make it happen in your own home.

RHINEBECK ANTIQUE SHOW

DUTCHESS COUNTY FAIRGROUNDS

6550 Spring Brook Avenue
Rhinebeck, New York 12572
rhinebeckantiquesfair.com
845-876-1989
The promoter of this long-running show in picturesque Rhinebeck, New York, has a knack for handpicking the best vendors! It's the place to go for exceptional period farmhouse finds and folk art.

NORTH CAROLINA

OLDE TYME MARKETPLACE

121 N White Street
Marshall, North Carolina 28103
704-942-6258
oldetymemarketplace.com
This twenty-year picker always has a great big farmhouse smile on her face. You can catch up with Beth Lewis at many antiques shows, like the City Farmhouse Pop-up Fair, but, when she's not on the road, you can visit her shop, where her focus is on farmhouse style all the way!

OHIO

COUNTRY LIVING FAIR COLUMBUS

Ohio Village
1982 Velma Avenue
Columbus, Ohio 43211
stellashows.com
September annually
The third of four annual shopping events hosted by

the shelter magazine of the same name, this fair takes place in the historic Ohio Village, making it right at home for a country showing of antiques and vintage.

SPRINGFIELD ANTIQUE EXTRAVAGANZA

Vintage Marketplace
Clark County Fairgrounds
4401 S. Charleston Pike
Springfield, Ohio 45505
springfieldantiqueshow.com
This is so much a favorite place of mine to pick for antiques and vintage, especially farmhouse style and architectural, that it should be a coveted secret. Consider yourself family that I'm sharing it with you.

OREGON

PLUCKY MAIDENS JUNK FEST!

Summer Junk Fest—Late July
Oaks Amusement Park
7805 SE Oaks Parkway
Portland, Oregon 97202
Holiday Junk Fest
Early November
Oregon Convention Center
Portland, Oregon
pluckymaidens.com
Each amazing Junk Fest hosts the best vendors in the northwest offering a smorgasbord of 100 percent pure, unadulterated Pluck! Plus the organizer of this event also hosts tours to Paris, London, and New York City. I think a Paris trip is in order. Anyone want to join me?

TENNESSEE

CITY FARMHOUSE

Yours Truly!
For all things City Farmhouse, including retail locations, the online shopping site, our Cross Country City Farmhouse on the Road Tour, and our annual Pop-up Fairs, book signings, and speaking engagements, visit our website.
cityfarmhousefranklin.com
615-268-0216

COUNTRY LIVING FAIR

James E. Ward Ag Center
945 E. Baddour Parkway
Lebanon, Tennessee 37087
stellashows.com
Nashville plays host to the first of four cross-country fairs presented by the shelter magazine of the same name. Antiques and vintage picks galore all in the nation's hotspot—Nashville, Tennessee!

NASHVILLE FLEA MARKET

Nashville Fairgrounds
625 Smith Avenue
Nashville, Tennessee 37203
nashvilleflea.com
Friday to Sunday, fourth weekend of each month
Pickers paradise in the home of Country Music! It's a large, awesome market with plenty of farmhouse-style goodness!

SOUTHERN JUNKER'S VINTAGE MARKET

Ag Center
7777 Walnut Groove Road
Memphis, Tennessee 38120
901-412-5485
Spring and fall annually
Held in the Land of the Delta Blues and Elvis! Yes, you should go! It's where southern junkers meet up, have fun, and shop for vintage and antiques.

GAS LAMP ANTIQUES

GAS LAMP ANTIQUES TOO

100 and 128 Powell Avenue
Nashville, Tennessee 37204
615-292-2250
Two fun spots to shop for upscale antiques and vintage. I always seem to find unique pieces for special design projects at these large malls.

THE NASHVILLE SHOW

Nashville Fairgrounds
625 Smith Avenue
Nashville, Tennessee 37203
tailgateantiqueshow.com
February annually
I'm not speaking lightly when I say that you will find the best in Americana antiques and vintage at this long-running show.

HIGH COTTON AND CO.

5021 Highway 412 N
Alamo, Tennessee 38001
731-345-3110
Catch up with Doris Lawrence at the City Farmhouse Pop-up Fair or in her shop just outside of Jackson, Tennessee. The style is farmhouse fabulous with many pieces having a local historical connection.

SCARLET SCALES ANTIQUES

246 2nd Avenue
Franklin, Tennessee 37064
615-791-4097
Scarlettscales.com
I have known Scarlett since she was a teenager, and she was selling antiques back then, too. Her shop is a lifestyle brand, offering antiques of all periods intermingled with contemporary pieces of the day. I never leave there without taking something away. Scarlett had a great teacher—her dad, Barry Scales, has been a picker for more than fifty years!

CR-71

230 Franklin Rd.
Factory at Franklin
Franklin, Tennessee 37064
615-293-5115
I really don't know where these guys pick for their shop, but I really wish I did! I've bought some of the most unusual things ever from Craig and Rick. They have helped me out on many decorating jobs, too. When I couldn't find enough farm tables for a restaurant design, they built them for me. The farm table in Sheryl Crow's writer's loft—yeah, they built that by hand.

THE SHOP AROUND THE CORNER

117 Third Ave. N
Franklin, Tennessee 37064
615-599-1652
Sometimes you need a painting, a rug, or an awesome throw pillow (or two, or three) to complete your farmhouse-style look. This shop is forever my go-to spot. That awesome ticking pillow on Rebecca Sweet's (Sweet Harmony) sofa, and the mound of luscious linen pillows on the gorgeous velvet tufted bed: Those all came from the Shop Around the Corner.

PHILLIPS GENERAL STORE

4 Railroad Square
Bell Buckle, Tennessee 37020
931-389-6547
Billy Phillips was born with an antique in his hand. If not, then he never left the delivery room without

one. If you love farmhouse, folk art, general store, or anything in between, then by all means go see Billy. On Halloween he seriously tricks out his shop windows. That alone is worth the trip.

TEXAS

TEXAS ANTIQUE WEEK

Spring and Fall
roundtop.org
Round Top, Warrenton, La Bahia, Burton, Brenham, and more tiny towns in between.
The granddaddy of them all, this antiquing hotspot is composed of more than fifty shows going on simultaneously over a two-and-a-half-week period. So, can you really see it all? No! Luckily for you, David and I have shopped this market for more than twenty years and we have curated the best pickin' spots to share with you.

Don't miss Marburger Farm Antique Show (seriously curated and very upscale) located in Round Top. From Round Top, you will want to shop the entire strip of fields from Marburger to Warrenton, including Zapp Hall, where you'll find everything from junk to fabulous farmhouse. It's a digger's and picker's paradise, so plan to stay a few days. Just past Warrenton, we always catch up with the amazing vendors at the historic Fayetteville Square. Prettiest little courthouse in Texas, by the way, and we never leave without having dinner at Joe's Place.

In the opposite direction from Round Top, hop on down the road to the La Bahia Antique Show and then to tiny little Burton, where several great shops (including Flown the Coop) are located. A short jaunt just past Burton is Leftovers Antiques, in Brenham. If you love period European antiques, then this is a must!

In Round Top, you'll want to make a stop at Bill Moore's large European antique warehouse. This is where you'll go to find multiples of farmhouse essentials, like old wooden buckets, galvanized tubs, demijohns in all sizes and colors, and fabulous doors, plus some surprises, too. It's amazing, some of the interesting pieces Bill brings in. It's always our first stop on the pickin' trail. You'll find him on the main road in Round Top—yeah, there's only one.

CHRISTIE'S

1023 Austin Avenue
Waco, Texas 76701
254-235-1047
Remember those very cool pillows on the faux leather sofa and the beautiful lush velvets that envelope the bed in the Made from Scratch loft in Waco, Texas? Christie custom-made those stunners! From her shop in Waco, she custom-makes bed coverings for home decorators all over the world. If you have something in mind for your own home, call her up; she'll design something special and hand-make it just for you.

ROOTS BOUTIQUE

201 S 2nd Street
Waco, Texas 76701
254-759-1771
Roots is a beautiful little lifestyle shop located in an historic building in downtown Waco. It's beautifully curated with antiques, vintage, and other homewares for a perfect farmhouse style. You can pick up an adorable outfit there as well. The awesome vintage Waco Hardware book styled on the coffee table in the Made from Scratch loft came from there.

UNCOMMON OBJECTS

1512 South Congress Avenue
Austin, Texas 78704
512-442-4000
uncommonobjects.com

In an effort to keep everything weird in Austin, this shop has gone above and beyond the call of duty. Just as the name implies, everything—and I do mean everything—in this shop is uncommon. One would expect no less from a shopkeeper who has a life-size cow over his awning at the entrance to the store.

ONLINE SHOPPING

FRENCHLARKSPUR.COM

Vintage French-inspired farmhouse living. This online shop offers plenty of the best curated pieces such as enamelware, old clocks, stoneware, period paintings, bread boards, ironstone, old letter bundles, house number plates, and more.

FLEAINGFRANCE.COM

A fabulous online shop for ironstone, transferware, sewing accessories, antique purses, candelabras, zinc, mannequins, religious compositions, silver, mirrors, paintings, chandeliers, school charts, copper, pharmacy bottles, books, and so much more.

ROUGHLINEN.COM

Beautifully woven coarse linens for the bed, table, upholstery, and more.

SCHOOLHOUSEELECTRIC.COM

Amazing period and modern lighting for any farmhouse-style space. The company now offers a complete home furnishings and accessories line.

HOMEDECORATORS.COM

Often, vintage or antique just won't do, especially when it comes to seating. Home Decorators is my favorite online haunt for affordable quality furnishings that work with a farmhouse-style aesthetic. They often offer free shipping, too!

DREAMYWHITES.COM

Beautifully curated antiques that inspire you to live an authentic farmhouse lifestyle. This online shop offers market baskets, soaps, wire caddies, baskets, ironstone, drying racks, even a French ticking dog bed!

VIVIETMARGOT.COM

Bringing a personal touch to French farmhouse living, this online site is curated and inspired by Charlotte Reiss's life in France. Here you will find beautiful canning jars, wooden spoons, linens, café au lait bowls, milk bottles, and more.

ANTIQUEAPPLIANCES.COM

If you are looking to add an authentic vibe to a kitchen, this is a source for it all! From stoves to refrigerators, this is your one-stop shop.

ACKNOWLEDGMENTS

TO GOD! THE GREATEST AUTHOR EVER KNOWN! You did it! All those many, many nights that I sat on my front porch and looked up to You in the heavens and prayed, *Take my hands, take my mind, and write this book*—You delivered! There wasn't a single day or night when I went back to the keyboard that You failed me. I am most humbled and grateful!

When I embarked on this journey to write *City Farmhouse Style*, I took my family with me. They sacrificed so much. My sweet husband, David, you slept so many nights alone and carried the burden of holding down the fort on all things City Farmhouse for what seems like forever! Little GuGu, thank you for being patient. I realize you missed so many Saturday nights at Mammie and Pawpaw's house. Lila, what can I say? I owe it all to you (or so you have told me so many times). It was that first meeting in New York that sealed the deal, right? Riley, you will never know how much it meant to me that you came to me that night at 1 AM (after I had been up for more than twenty-four hours straight) and offered to help. You helped me as only you know how: by sitting right beside me to keep me from being alone. To my mom, who likely worked way too many hours while I was on the road and writing my butt off. To say thank you to all of you just isn't enough.

To my amazing photographer, Alissa Saylor: Your talents for bringing *City Farmhouse Style* to life are beyond extraordinary! You not only looked behind the camera; you looked through my eyes and into my mind (and that alone is pretty scary). You nailed it! Together we have inspired farmhouse-style lovers all over the world! You should be proud!

Sandra Soria and Caroline McKenzie, there are no words to express my gratitude for your collaboration to make this happen. Your inspiration, your dedication, and the countless hours you spent behind this project helped bring it all home! You two are superstars!

To my former editor at Random House, P J Dempsey, thank you for reeling me in over and over! There were many times I wanted to throw in the towel, but your encouragement and knowledge of all things "publishing" kept me going!

To my agent, Marilyn Allen, thank you for a job well done! Let's do this again!

To Robelyn at Redneck Chic, Christie's in Waco, Texas, and Roots in Waco, Texas: You came to the rescue in a huge way! I'm so grateful for you all!

Debbie and Danny (aka Cat Daddy), a girl can't make it without her backup! Thank you for always being there! Georgie Daniel, thank you for all your help in getting many of these homes ready for the camera and then putting it all back together. Patina Green in McKinney, what you guys are making over there is insane! Thanks so much for feeding us!

Ruth Barnes, I love you! You have been my dearest friend and my biggest cheerleader!

Many xos to my hometown girl and brilliant writer, Rachel Hardage Barrett, who penned the most beautiful foreword ever written—thank you!

Many hugs to photographer Nicole Franzen, whose eye behind the camera captured the true beauty of a brownstone in Brooklyn.

To my rock star publisher, ABRAMS, and all the amazing staff who worked tirelessly on this project! In particular: Shawna Mullen, you are the sweetest, kindest soul. I knew right away we were going to be like family. I mean that and I love you! xoxoxo. To Sarah Gifford, you are a design star! The way you work your magic brings it all to life. To Gabe Levinson, Danny Maloney, and Rebecca Westall, every successful project requires top-notch managers. Grateful to have the best!

To all the amazing homeowners across America: Laurie and Chris Popp, Cindy Williams, Odette Williams and Nick Law, Allison Murphy, Martha and Bryan Thomas, Theodore Leaf and Matthew Habib, Debbie Fishman and Tim Meyn, Andrea and Ryan Geibel, Rebecca and Phillip Sweet, Lindsay and Jamey Hines, Lucy and Conner Farmer, Sheryl Crow, Tanya and Matthew Cross, and Kimberly Kelly. How grateful I am that you so graciously opened your doors, so that we all can be inspired by what makes your home uniquely City Farmhouse style.

To all of our many, many City Farmhouse supporters (customers, design clients, Facebook, Instagram, blog, and email followers) who love farmhouse style as much as we do. This book is possible because of you! It was you who helped shape this design style called City Farmhouse style! xos for life!

Many ((((hugs)))) to Molly Howard, who on that shoot in Birmingham, Alabama, whipped up the most amazing homemade lunches ever!

To Maxwell House Coffee, for 3,164 good-to-the-last-drop cups! Yes, I was counting!

And last but certainly not least, Minnie Ola'Belle Harness, my grandmother, Momma, who was country when country wasn't cool!

ABOUT THE AUTHOR

KIM LEGGETT is a designer, antiques and vintage dealer, and author. She and her husband, David, own City Farmhouse, an online and retail interior design destination; The Fling, a monthly antiques and vintage sale event; and The City Farmhouse Pop-up Fair, held in June and October in Franklin, Tennessee—which draws thousands of shoppers from across the United States and Canada, and is listed as one of the Top Five Events in the South by *Southern Living* magazine.

Kim's interior design work has been featured in *Architectural Digest*, *Country Living*, *Flea Market Style*, and numerous other publications.

cityfarmhousefranklin.com

EDITOR SHAWNA MULLEN

DESIGNER SARAH GIFFORD

PRODUCTION MANAGER REBECCA WESTALL

Library of Congress Control Number: 2016960600

ISBN: 978-1-4197-2650-7

Printed and bound in U.S.A.
10 9 8 7 6 5 4 3 2 1

54

126